James M. Stephenson, P. T. Russell

**A Report of a Public Discussion between J. M. Stephenson and P. T. Russell**

Subject: The Kingdom of God upon Earth

James M. Stephenson, P. T. Russell

**A Report of a Public Discussion between J. M. Stephenson and P. T. Russell**
*Subject: The Kingdom of God upon Earth*

ISBN/EAN: 9783337184230

Printed in Europe, USA, Canada, Australia, Japan

Cover: Foto ©ninafisch / pixelio.de

More available books at **www.hansebooks.com**

# A REPORT

## OF A

# PUBLIC DISCUSSION

BETWEEN

## J. M. STEPHENSON AND P. T. RUSSELL.

SUBJECT:

## THE KINGDOM OF GOD UPON EARTH;

ITS NATURE, LOCALITY, THE TIME OF ITS ESTABLISHMENT, AND ITS
DURATION, AS TAUGHT BY THE PROPHETS,
CHRIST AND HIS APOSTLES.

---

Old Union, Ind., September 28th to October 3d, 1866.

REPORTED BY C. W. STAGG, OF INDIANAPOLIS.

---

INDIANAPOLIS:
DOWNEY & BROUSE, PRINTERS.
1866.

Entered according to Act of Congress, in the year of our Lord 1867, by
JAMES M. STEPHENSON,
In the Clerk's Office of the District Court of the United States for the District of Indiana.

# REPORT
#### OF A
# PUBLIC DISCUSSION,
##### BETWEEN
### J. M. STEPHENSON AND P. T. RUSSELL—HELD AT OLD UNION, IND., SEPTEMBER 25-28, 1866.

##### QUESTION:

*Resolved,* That the kingdom of God, spoken of in Dan. ii: 44, was set up on the Day of Pentecost, spoken of in Acts, 2d chapter.

## AFF.—P. T. RUSSELL—FIRST SPEECH.

FIRST SESSION, Tuesday Morning, 10 o'clock.

*Gentlemen Moderators, Brethren and Friends:—*

WE now approach this important proposition — the query—is, or is not, the "kingdom" spoken of by Daniel in the second chapter and forty-fourth verse, of his prophecy already set up, and has it been set up ever since the day of Pentecost? There is more involved in this question than at first blush may appear. The entire ground already passed over is directly involved in this issue, for if we prove the affirmative, viz: that the kingdom spoken of in Daniel, 2d chapter, and 44th verse, was set up on the day of Pentecost, and consequently that the servants of the Lord under the gospel system are now receiving and enjoying it, being thus set up, then we know beyond the possibility of a doubt, that they shall possess that kingdom "forever and ever." Permit me therefore to invite your attention directly to the language contained in the chapter and verse named—Daniel 2d chapter and 44th verse. It is as follows: "And in the days of these kings shall the God of heaven set up a kingdom, which shall never be destroyed: and the kingdom shall not be left to other people, but it shall break in pieces and consume all these kingdoms, and it shall stand forever."

On this declaration of the inspired prophet is based the proposition before us. It now devolves upon me to call your attention to the leading terms of the proposition. And first, we have the term "kingdom" and not only the term "kingdom," but the term "kingdom of God,"—a divine government, unlike anything that had ever gone before it—which was at the period spoken of to be set up. Not only so, but we have also the term "set up" here, and it is the only instance in which that term is found in connection with the word "kingdom." These words, "set up" are identical in meaning with the words "erect" and "establish."

It remains for us in the next place, to read the declaration contained in the first verse of the second chapter of the Acts of the Apostles: "And when the day of Pentecost was fully come, they were all with one accord in one place." Here we have an allusion to the time and the occasion upon which our proposition affirms the kingdom spoken of in Daniel 2d chapter and 44th verse, to have been set up.

Having thus the terms embraced in the proposition clearly before us, let us go to Daniel 7th chapter, 13th and 14th verses, where we find the following language: "I saw in the night visions, and behold, one like the Son of man came with the clouds of heaven, and came to the Ancient of days, and they brought him near before him."

"And there was given him dominion, and glory, and a kingdom, that all people, nations, and languages should serve him: his dominion is an everlasting dominion, which shall not pass away, and his kingdom that which shall not be destroyed."

Here we have an allusion to the same kingdom spoken of in Daniel 2d chapter and 44th verse. In the 2d chapter and 44th verse, it is said of this kingdom that it "shall never be destroyed," and in the 14th verse of the 7th chapter it is asserted that "his dominion is an everlasting dominion, which shall not pass away, and his kingdom that which shall not be destroyed," thus identifying the two places as speaking of one and the same kingdom. But in looking again at Daniel 2d chapter and 44th verse, we find that "the kingdom shall not be left to other people." Bearing this in mind, let us pass and observe the assertion found in Daniel 7th chapter and 18th verse: "But the saints of the most high shall take the kingdom, and possess the kingdom forever, even forever and ever," which is equivalent to the phrase, "the kingdom shall not be left to other people," found in Daniel, 2d chapter and 44th verse.

Having said thus much for the purpose of identifying the two passages as speaking in regard to one and the same kingdom, let us next inquire what are the ordinary and the essential elements of a kingdom? and while I ask what are the essential elements of a kingdom, I answer as follows: first, a king, crowned, clothed with authority; second, as a result his issuing laws; third, subjects submitting to those laws thus issued. Wherever we have these three elements conjoined there we find a kingdom, and wherever these three elements meet, there we find the beginning of a kingdom. To these three points then we shall call your attention. But first I desire to bring before your minds some further testimony upon this point. Go with me now to Revelations 19th chapter, and let us scan it for one moment. I will read the 11th and 16th verses inclusive. "And I saw heaven opened, and behold a white horse; and he that sat upon him was called faithful and true, and in righteousness he doth judge and make war." "And he hath on his vesture and on his thigh a name written, KING OF KINGS, AND LORD OF LORDS."

Mark the language contained in the 16th verse: "And

he hath on his vesture and on his thigh a name written, KING OF KINGS, AND LORD OF LORDS." Here we have the Messiah identified. John says: "I saw heaven opened" and then follows a description of a certain glorious being whom he saw within that heaven and who is partially described in these words: "he was clothed in a vesture dipped in blood," and if there was any further description of his person it would point directly to that one spoken of by Isaiah, as "a man of sorrows and acquainted with grief." And the concluding part of the same verse tells us that "his name is called The Word of God." Mark his titles — he has on his vesture and on his thigh a name written, "King of Kings, and Lord of Lords"—titles that can not mean one jot or tittle less than a king supreme in himself. This John saw in a vision. He saw him with these titles there, and if John told the truth when he said he saw him justly wearing these titles, then he is now, even at this very hour KING OF KINGS, AND LORD OF LORDS, and if he is now thus "King of Kings, and Lord of Lords," it is because he is even now on the throne promised him —it is because that "kingdom" spoken of in Daniel, 2d chapter and 44th verse is already in existence.

Let me call attention to some further testimony. Go with me to Colossians, 1st Chapter, and 13th verse, which we will read thus: "Who hath delivered you from the power of darkness, and hath translated *you* into the Kingdom of his dear Son." I believe I have made a mistake of one word in reading this verse, using the word "you" instead of the word "us." Reading it correctly, we have the Apostle Paul, (speaking of the Lord,) saying: "Who hath delivered *us* from the power of darkness, and hath translated *us* into the Kingdom of his dear Son." I pause here for one moment to remark that the same Greek word which is here rendered translated, is the identical word used in Hebrews, 11th Chapter, where it is said that Enoch was *translated*. Here they are spoken of as being "delivered from the power of darkness, and translated into the Kingdom of God's dear Son." Now, they were, that is to say, Paul and those included with him in the word "us," were either then introduced into the Kingdom of God's dear Son, or they were not. If they were not at the time Paul penned that sentence, introduced into the Kingdom of God's dear Son, then the record is erroneous. If they were then introduced into that Kingdom, that Kingdom was then in existence, and if it was in existence it was "set up." If it was not "set up" it was not in existence; if it was not in existence it was simply nothing, and if it was nothing then the Apostle Paul and all of his brethren were entered into nothing according to Colossians, 1st Chapter and 13th verse.

Let us look at one passage more in connection with this thought. Go with me to Hebrews, 12th Chapter and 28th verse. It reads as follows: "Wherefore, we receiving a Kingdom which cannot be moved, let us have grace, whereby we may serve God acceptably, with reverence. and Godly fear."

There are several thoughts connected with this expression of the Apostle. Look if you please carefully at the words, "cannot be moved," and compare this statement of the Apostle with Daniel, 2nd Chapter, and 44th verse. "shall never be destroyed," and we find that the Prophet and the Apostle in these two sentences express the same thought precisely. But in Hebrews, 12th Chapter and 28th verse, the Apostle avers of himself and his brethren, and having reference to the same kingdom spoken of in Daniel, 2nd Chapter and 44th verse, that they were at that very time receiving it. Mark the force of the present participle, "we *receiving* a kingdom which cannot be moved." Now, they were either receiving it, or they were not; if they were, it was in existence; if they were not, then we have here, from the pen of the Apostle Paul, language entirely unjustifiable and erroneous; for I am very well aware, and so are you, that the idea of the reception by any body of a mere nonentity is simply ridiculous.

Having thus glanced over the foreground of this subject, let us pass to Daniel, 2nd Chapter, and notice briefly several expressions that are contained therein. The 34th and 35th verses of this Chapter read as follows:

"Thou sawest till that a stone was cut out without hands, which smote the image upon his feet *that were* of iron and clay, and brake them to pieces. Then was the iron, the clay, the brass, the silver, and the gold broken to pieces together, and became like the chaff of the summer threshing floors; and the wind carried them away, that no place was found for them: and the stone that smote the image became a great mountain, and filled the whole earth."

The first thought that I want to fasten here is this: the stone here spoken of, which became a great mountain and filled the whole earth, is the emblem of a kingdom and that kingdom spoken of in the 44th verse of the same chapter:

"And in the days of these kings shall the God of heaven set up a kingdom, which shall never be destroyed: and the kingdom shall not be left to other people, *but* it shall break in pieces and consume all these kingdoms, and it shall stand for ever. Forasmuch as thou sawest that the stone was cut out of the mountain without hands, and that it brake in pieces the iron, the brass, the clay, the silver and the gold; the great God hath made known to the king what shall come to pass hereafter; and the dream *is* certain, and the interpretation thereof sure."

Let us pass to notice the circumstances under which Daniel appeared before the king. The king had had a very unusual dream, that had so far gone from him that he could not apprehend it clearly and distinctly. There were those around him who laid claims to super-human wisdom and ability. They claimed not only the power of looking into the future and foretelling events that were yet to come, but they also claimed the power of looking into the past, examining its dark scroll and telling to mortal ear the secret things that had been. They claimed also the power of scanning the hidden recesses of the human heart, and telling to the world what was passing there. The king concludes that now is a good time to test the skill of these men. He calls them into his presence and tells them what has occurred, and demands of them the solution of the problem. They exclaim, "O,

King, live forever! Tell thy servants the dream and we will shew the interpretations." The king says to them: "If you can tell the interpretations of the dream you can also tell the dream itself." They reply to him, "O, King, we cannot tell." In anger, he exclaims, "If you do not accomplish this, death is the certain doom of every one of you." In deep dejection they slowly depart. The executioner proceeds with the preparations for his deadly work. He approaches the quarter where Daniel is. Daniel approaches the executioner exclaiming, "Why is the king's decree so hasty?" The executioner related the circumstances, and Daniel went to the king and asked that time might be given him, promising to reveal the dream and the interpretation thereof. Time is granted. "Then was the secret revealed to Daniel in a night vision." See Daniel now appearing before the king in the simple majesty of truth and honest conviction. He says:

"Thou, O king, sawest, and behold a great image. This great image, whose brightness was excellent, stood before thee; and the form thereof was terrible. This image's head was of fine gold, his breast and his arms of silver, his belly and his thighs of brass, his legs of iron, his feet part of iron and part of clay. Thou sawest till that a stone was cut out without hands, which smote the image upon his feet that were of iron and clay, and brake them to pieces. Then was the iron, the clay, the brass, the silver, and the gold, broken to pieces together, and became like the chaff of the summer threshing floors; and the wind carried them away, that no place was found for them: and the stone that smote the image became a great mountain, and filled the whole earth."

Daniel says to the King, This is the dream, and now I will tell you what it means. Thou, O, King, art this head of gold; after thee shall rise another kingdom, inferior to thee in splendor as silver is inferior to gold; a third kingdom shall supercede that, still more inferior, less wealthy, as brass is less valuable than silver. After that kingdom shall have passed away, a fourth kingdom shall arise, emblematized by the iron. Here, now, we have four kingdoms, and only four, spoken of in the premises; first, the Assyrian, indicated by the head of gold; second, the Medo-Persian; third, the Grecian, under Alexander the Great, which was superceded by that of the Romans, under the Cæsars. Now, says Daniel, in the 44th verse: "In the days of these Kings shall the God of Heaven set up a Kingdom." Mark the force of the word "these," pointing specifically and pointedly to what is found in the premises, and in immediate connection with it, and meaning neither more nor less than the Kings last mentioned in the context going before—"In the days of *these Kings* shall the God of Heaven set up a Kingdom." If the term had been intended to apply to something far off, then the term "those" would have been employed instead of the term "these." "These," as you well know, always points to the things more near, and "those" to the things that are farther off.

While thus glancing at the meaning of the term here employed, the term "these," mark, in connection with it, the language of the 42d verse:

"And as the toes of the feet were part of iron and part of clay, so the *kingdoms* shall be partly strong and partly broken."

Did I read that verse correctly? I will read it again precisely as I read it before:

"And as the toes of the feet were part of iron and part of clay, so the *kingdoms* shall be partly strong and partly broken."

I read it incorrectly, and I did so for the simple purpose of fastening upon your minds the truth that there is but one kingdom here spoken of, the word used being "kingdom," singular, and not "kingdoms," plural. Unless ten kingdoms can be represented by the singular number, and called "kingdom" simply, then we cannot, with any show of propriety go to a conversation that occurred a long time afterwards, recorded in the 7th chapter of Daniel, and make this word "kingdom," used in the passage before us, refer to the ten kingdoms that arose out of the ruins of the Roman Empire. And while thus we have the term "kingdom" used here in the singular number, observe also that it is said that they shall not cleave together, even as iron is not mixed with clay. And then follows the language recorded in the 44th and 45th verses. "And in the days of these kings shall the God of heaven set up a kingdom which shall never be destroyed: and the kingdom shall not be left to other people, but shall break in pieces and consume all these kingdoms, and it shall stand forever." "Forasmuch as thou sawest that the stone was cut out of the mountain without hands, and that it break in pieces the iron, the brass, the clay, the silver, and the gold; the great God hath made known to the king what shall come to pass hereafter: and the dream is certain, and the interpretation thereof sure."

The special thought which I wish to fasten here is the simple truth that the kingdom here emblematized by a stone is said to be cut out of a mountain. A mountain in prophetic imagery commonly represents a kingdom. The kingdom represented by the stone must therefore have been cut of the kingdom represented by the mountain, before the mountain was leveled to the plain. Secondly, as it was cut out of the old Jewish kingdom, as a natural consequence it must have been cut out before the demolition of that organic, political body, before the Jews had ceased to be an embodied people, before their final dispersion by the Roman armies under Vespasian and his son Titus. Since that time they have been dispersed abroad over the whole face of the earth, and there has been nothing about them to fulfil the idea of a kingdom. Once they were a mountain, but now they have become a plain. As the stone was cut out of the mountain it must have been taken out during the period of their ac-actual national existence, and before their dispersion.

In connection with these thoughts I call your attention to Micah, 4th chapter. Examine the language contained in the first verse: "But in the last days it shall come to pass, that the mountain of the house of the LORD shall be established in the top of the mountains, and it shall be exalted above the hills; and people shall flow unto it."

Here the same kingdom is represented by the idea of a mountain, "the mountain of the Lord's house," and it is said to be set up and established in the top of the mountain, "in the last days." Last days of what? That is the important point here to be decided? In answer to this important inquiry turn now to the preceding chapter, the third chapter of Micah and read the language therein contained, commencing at the 9th verse and including the remainder of the chapter.

"Hear this, I pray you, ye heads of the house of Jacob, and princes of the house of Israel, and abhor judgment, and pervert all equity." "They build up Zion with blood, and Jerusalem with iniquity." "The heads thereof judge for reward, and the priests thereof teach for hire, and the prophets thereof divine for money; yet will they lean upon the LORD, and say, Is not the LORD among us? none evil can come upon us." "Therefore shall Zion, for your sake be ploughed as a field, and Jerusalem shall become heaps, and the mountain of the house as the high places of the forest."

## NEG.—J. M. STEPHENSON—FIRST SPEECH.

I appear before you in order to investigate this important issue—an issue not only between my opponent and myself, but also between us as a people and all other professed churches of God in the world, in some essential feature. But while this is the case, there is at the same time one point at issue between the church of my opponent and that to which I belong, almost exclusively, it is the position that the "kingdom is the church" that was set up on the day of Pentecost. The church to which he belongs is the only one in Christendom which occupies the position that the kingdom of God, spoken of in the passage of scripture named in the proposition before us, was set up on the day of Pentecost. He and his church stand alone upon this point. In the statement that was made by my opponent, that the question at issue between us was in effect, whether the kingdom of God spoken of in the 44th verse of the 2d chapter of Daniel "*is* or is *not*" now set up, he did not state the issue as it really is. That is not the issue between us. The issue is—was the kingdom of God spoken of in Daniel, 2d chapter and 44th verse, set up on the day of Pentecost. And if therefore it can be shown that that kingdom was set up either previously or subsequently to the day of Pentecost, it is evident to every mind that my opponent loses the question at issue between us. I propose in this investigation to follow the example of my opponent in the investigation of the former question, and to prove the negative of this question antecedently—we both have the affirmative in this case. He affirms that the kingdom alluded to in Daniel 2d chapter and 44th verse, was set up on the day of Pentecost—we on the other hand affirm that this event is yet future. From that point forward, from the establishment of the kingdom on, I think we shall not differ from each other, but shall agree that the kingdom, whenever set up, shall endure forever.

I propose in the first place to investigate the harmonious teachings of the word of God in reference to the *nature* of the Kingdom of God, the *time* when the Kingdom of God will be established, and all the *essential* elements of the Kingdom as revealed in the word of God, and prove to you and to all who shall read this discussion, that the establishment of the Kingdom of God is a future event; and that the view held by us as a people, in regard to the *time* when that Kingdom shall be set up is the only one that will harmonize the Holy Scriptures—that the whole Bible, from Genesis to Revelations, harmonize perfectly and entirely with our view of the subject, and that all the proofs that are produced, or sought to be produced by my opponent, are only so many *objections* to the harmonious teachings of the word of God. I shall treat them just as I would treat objections urged by an infidel, or by any other class of men, to the plain and harmonious teachings of divine inspiration. One word just here in reference to the rules by which we are governed in the investigation of the word of God. We do not investigate or construe the word of God by isolated texts. We investigate by subjects. We do not suspend our faith upon a few passages of Scripture, wrested from their proper and legitimate relation with the context, but upon the harmonious teachings of the entire word of God. We will advocate no view, we will subscribe to no doctrine, we will acknowledge no sentiment upon which we cannot harmonize the teachings of the whole Bible. If I cannot harmonize our views with the word of God, it will clearly prove one of two things—either that we have not the truth upon our side, or that I have not the intellectual ability to make that truth appear.

I wish to state to you here in the outset what are the essential elements of every kingdom that has been set up on this globe of ours, from the time when Nimrod, the mighty hunter, set up his kingdom, down to the present time, viz:—first, a *king;* secondly, *subjects;* thirdly, *associate rulers* with the king. No king or potentate has ever ruled the world alone. All the monarchs of the earth have their Cabinets, their associates in authority who share with them the responsibility and the royalty of the kingdom. And if, in the Kingdom of God that is to come, we are not to have associated with the ruling Monarch of that Kingdom, a royal Cabinet, it will be an exception to the general rule. But I was going on to state that in the fourth place there must be a *territory.* Every kingdom on the face of the earth possesses its territory. A kingdom is an organic body, and can no more exist without a territory than any super-structure without a foundation. The Kingdom of God therefore must have a locality and a territory. In the fifth place it must have a *capital.* All other kingdoms have had their capitals, their great political centres from which have radiated laws for the government of the kingdom or empire. The Kingdom of God must likewise have its capital, or be an exception. In the sixth place it must have laws to bind the extremities of the Kingdom to the centre; otherwise it would not be an organic body. There is no necessity to make the Kingdom of God an exception to all other kingdoms with reference to any of these six essential elements, and if I can demonstrate, by the harmonious teachings of the word of God, that the Kingdom here promised to be set up by the God of Heaven and given to Jesus Christ, is the only Kingdom that God has ever promised to His Son, or which He ever will establish permanently and forever on the earth, then that Kingdom will, in common with all other kingdoms, possess these six essential elements; and if I can prove this, my opponent can show no necessity for spiritualizing any of these elements. And if we can show the literal fulfillment of all the promises made in the word of God concerning Christ's Kingdom, no man has any right to place a spiritual construction upon any of them. If we can trace an analogy between the Kingdom of God and all other kingdoms, then my opponent can make no show of consistency in refusing to understand the word of God according to its literal import, and for interpreting the Kingdom of God, here spoken of, as not having promised these six fundamental and essential elements of a kingdom.

My first postulate, in entering upon this subject, is: that it was God's original purpose, when he made man, to constitute him, on condition of obedience, his vicegerent, to administer his government on the earth forever and ever. Go back with me now, and let us investigate the great charter, the original charter of all legal rights and of all authority which man can exercise upon this earth. It is found in Genesis, 1st Chapter and 26th verse.

"And God said, Let us make man in our image, after our likeness; and let them have dominion over the fish of the sea, and over the fowl of the air, and over the cattle, and over all the earth, and over every creeping thing that creepeth upon the earth."

The dominion of the whole earth was the kingdom that the great God promised to Adam, and in proof that this proffered dominion was identical with the Kingdom promised to Jesus Christ by all the prophets that ever wrote under the influence of divine inspiration. See Matthew, 25th Chapter, commencing at the 31st verse:

"When the Son of man shall come in his glory, and all the holy angels with him, then shall he sit upon the throne of his glory: and before him shall be gathered all nations: and he shall separate them one from another, as a shepherd divideth *his* sheep from the goats: and he shall set the sheep on his right hand, but the goats on the left. Then shall the King say unto them on his right hand, Come, ye blessed of my Father, inherit the kingdom prepared for you from the foundation of the world."

Go back with me to the time when the foundations of the earth were laid, when "the morning stars sang together, and all the sons of God shouted for joy," and learn what kingdom was *then* and *there* prepared for man. In the 1st Chapter of Genesis and the 26th verse we find this language: "Let us make man, and let them have dominion over all the earth."

In the next place, that this dominion spoken of here was designed to be perpetual in case of obedience, is evident from the fact that God declared that in case of disobedience they should surely die. Look at the following language used by the Divine Being after Adam's criminality, and after his sentence was passed upon him by his Creator. God says of the guilty criminal: "Behold, the man is become as one of us, to know good and evil: and now, lest he put forth his hand and take also of the tree of life, and eat and live for ever: therefore, the Lord God sent him forth from the garden of Eden, to till the ground from whence he was taken." Genesis, 3d Chapter, 22d and 23d verses. We see at once from this that God in His original plan, offered Adam, in connection with the promised throne of universal empire, the everlasting possession of the earth. All this was promised to Adam on condition of obedience. By his disobedience he forfeited that right.

The second Adam came. To him was offered the endless kingdom of God, upon precisely the same terms on which it had been offered to the first Adam—Christ came "to seek and to save that which was lost." Did the second Adam comply with the conditions on which the endless dominion of earth was promised? He did. "All my father's commandments" said Christ, "I have kept." He invites the blessed of his Father to come and share with him "the kingdom prepared for them from the foundation of the world." It was the kingdom prepared and designed for man, when the foundations of the earth were laid. The first Adam having proved disobedient and recreant to his trust, the second Adam came, and to him was promised the same kingdom which the first Adam had forfeited through disobedience, and upon the same terms. The second Adam fulfilled all the conditions of the grant and to him is promised the same everlasting kingdom and dominion that was originally promised to the first Adam.

Again we find the Almighty after the flood had swept the earth with the besom of destruction, revealing his purposes in regard to his government upon the earth. Turn to the 17th chapter of Genesis and we there find God making a covenant with his servant Abraham which he calls "an everlasting covenant." What is the import of the promise there made by Jehovah to Abraham? Does he not say? "I will give to thee and to thy seed an everlasting possession in the land of Canaan." He names the land—"all the land of Canaan." See Gen. xvii: 1—8 "And when Abram was ninety years old and nine, the Lord appeared to Abram, and said unto him, I am the Almighty God; walk before me and be thou perfect." And I will make my covenant between me and thee, and will multiply thee exceedingly. And Abram fell on his face; and God talked with him saying. As for me, behold, my covenant is with thee, and thou shalt be a father of many nations. Neither shall thy name any more be called Abram, but thy name shall be Abraham; for a father of many nations have I made thee. And I will make thee exceeding fruitful, and I will make nations of thee, and kings shall come out of thee. And I will establish my covenant between me and thee and thy seed after thee in their generations, for an everlasting covenant, to be a God unto thee and to thy seed after thee. And I will give unto thee, and to thy seed after thee, the land wherein thou art a stranger, all the land of Canaan, for an everlasting possession; and I will be their God."

In the 22d chapter of Genesis, and at the 17th and 18th verses, we find God making another promise to Abraham in these words: "That in blessing I will bless thee, and in multiplying I will multiply thy seed as the stars of heaven, and as the sand which is upon the sea shore; and thy seed shall possess the gate of his enemies: And in thy seed shall all the nations of the earth be blessed; because thou hast obeyed my voice."

Observe here that the possessive pronoun "his" is used in the singular number, and cannot correctly represent a multitude as numerous as the "stars of heaven" and the "sands upon the sea shore."

By referring to the 12th chapter of Genesis we find the same promise made to Abraham; "In thee shall all the families of the earth be blessed." In the 26th chapter of Genesis we find the same promise recapitulated to Isaac —that in him and in his seed should all the nations of the earth be blessed, and that the Almighty would give the land to the seed of Abraham for an everlasting possession.

Turn now to the 12th and 14th verses inclusive of the 28th chapter of Genesis. I will read it *verbatim;* Jacob is here upon his journey into a foreign country, flying from the anger and power of his elder brother, Esau. Lying on the cold earth, with a stone for his pillow, and the starry heavens for a canopy above him, he is dreaming a strange dream. He sees in the visions of the night a ladder reaching from heaven to earth. It presented the means of a possible passage between the two worlds, for angels were ascending and descending upon it. "And behold the Lord God," &c. "And he dreamed, and behold a ladder set up on the earth, and the top of it reached to heaven; and behold the angels of God ascending and descending on it. And behold, the Lord stood above it, and said, I am the Lord God of Abraham thy father, and the God of Isaac; the land whereon thou liest, to thee will I give it, and to thy seed. And thy seed shall be as the dust of the earth; and thou shalt spread abroad to the west, and to the east, and to the north, and to the south; and in thee and in thy seed shall all the families of the earth be blessed."

Observe this language with care. What does the Lord God, standing at the top of this miraculous ladder say to Jacob? Does he say: "Jacob, come up here, for all heaven will I give to thee and thy seed forever?" No such language does he use. On the contrary he says, "Jacob, *the land whereon thou liest*, to thee will I give it and to thy seed." Hence we see that it was God's purpose to give them the land of Canaan for an everlasting possession, as a centre from which should radiate laws for the government of the world to all eternity. This land was in the first place, to be given them. Secondly the area of the whole earth, the government of the entire earth was to be given them, as involved in the promise made to Abraham. "In thee and in thy seed shall all the nations of the earth be blessed." Now who were associated with Abraham, Isaac and Jacob in this immutable title to the dominion of the whole earth, backed up by the oath of Almighty God? I will now introduce to you our brother in Christ Jesus, the great Paul, a man of transcendent ability and taught at the feet of Gamaliel, the greatest lawyer of the age in which he lived. Hear him—hear Paul's immutable testimony to the important truth before us. What does Paul say? We have his testimony in the 3d chapter of Galatians, at the 16th verse. "Now to Abraham and his seed were the promises made. He saith not, And to seeds, as of many; but as of one, and to thy seed, which is Christ." To Abraham and to Christ, then, these glorious promises were made. The last verse of the same chapter tells us, "And if ye be Christ's then are ye Abraham's seed and heirs according to the promise."

## AFF.—P. T. RUSSELL—SECOND SPEECH.

I desire to commence where I concluded—to finish the argument I had begun when my time expired—and after that to review the argument that you have just listened to. I will call your attention once more to the third chapter of Micah—I will commence reading at the ninth verse:

"Hear this, I pray you, ye heads of the house of Jacob, and princes of the house of Israel, that abhor judgment, and pervert all equity. They build up Zion with blood, and Jerusalem with iniquity. The heads thereof judge for reward, and the priests thereof teach for hire, and the prophets thereof divine for money: yet will they lean upon the Lord, and say, is not the Lord among us? none evil can come upon us. Therefore, shall Zion for your sake be plowed as a field, and Jerusalem shall become heaps, and the mountain of the house as the high places of the forest. But in the last days it shall come to pass, that the mountain of the house of the Lord shall be established in the top of the mountains, and it shall be exalted above the hills; and the people shall flow unto it."

I have read this language for the simple purpose of fastening upon your minds the time indicated in the words, "last days." I had sprung the question, "Last days" of what? Look at the context. Here I shuold remind you that the division of the Scriptures into chapters and verses, is a matter of modern origin, and formed no part whatever of the divine arrangement. And here we find the prophet Micah, in the fore part of the fourth chapter of his prophecies which we have read in your hearing, predicting certain matters that transpired as a result from the overthrow and destruction of the city of Jerusalem, and of her temple, which overthrow was described in the last concluding portion of the chapter going before. When the city of Jerusalem was overthrown the temple was prostrated; the very foundations thereof were overturned, the Roman plowshares making furrows on the ground where it had stood, thus indicating the fact that it should never again be built. Hence the language found in the last verse of the third chapter—"Zion shall be plowed as a field." Then immediately following, in the first verses of the fourth chapter, we have certain events named which were to transpire "in the last days." The idea evidently is, that in the last days of Jerusalem, a short time before the demolition of the temple and the dispersion of the Jews among all nations, "the mountain of the Lord's house" should be "established in the top of the mountains." This language you will at once observe is in perfect accord with that of Daniel, 2d chapter, 4th verse, "in the days of these kings." We shall see, by and by, that it was in the days of the Roman Cesars that the God of Heaven should set up the Kingdom spoken of in the language before us.

Here let us pause and examine one statement made by my friend here. He stated that upon the one single point of the unity of God's Kingdom he was willing to suspend the entire issue between us. It is a matter of curiosity with me to see how he can make the Kingdom of God to be "set up" in "the last days," or "in the days of these kings," long after time had been rolling its ceaseless changes round, and yet, at the same time assert that the kingdom, the same kingdom (there being only one,) was established "when the morning stars sang together." You were told that the second Adam took the place in God's design which had been forfeited by the first. The first Adam had dominion over all the brute creation. That was his dominion, and now, therefore, if the second Adam takes the place the first occupied, then will he, the Lord Jesus Christ, have dominion over the brutes; and if so, then, as a natural consequence, mankind are not now, and never will be, under any obligations to obey and serve him. The Psalmist says, "Thou madest him to have dominion over the fowls of the air, and over the fish of the sea, and whatsoever passeth through the paths of the sea." Here is David's understanding of the nature of the dominion given to the first Adam. If, therefore, my friend has told you the truth when he said that the second Adam took the place of the first, then the dominion of the Lord Jesus Christ cannot go beyond the limits of Adam's dominion, and therefore is confined to the brutes, and has nothing to do with you or with me.

I now desire to call your minds back to the argument upon which I had entered when my time expired. Let us return and look at the prophecies and their fulfillment for the purpose of marking the time of the coronation of the King. Go with me first to 2d Samuel, 7th chapter, 12th and 17th verses inclusive.

"And when thy days be fulfilled, and thou shalt sleep with thy fathers, I will set up thy seed after thee, which shall proceed out of thy bowels, and I will establish his kingdom. He shall build a house for my name, and I will establish the throne of his kingdom for ever. I will be his father, and he shall be my son. If he commit iniquity, I will chasten him with the rod of men, and with the stripes of the children of men: but my mercy shall not depart away from him, as I took it from Saul, whom I put away before thee. And thine house and thy kingdom shall be established forever before thee: thy throne shall be established forever. According to all these words, and according to all this vision, so did Nathan speak unto David."

Mark one matter: here is a promise that that throne called "the throne of David" should be established forever; it should not pass away; and not only this, but that his descendants should forever reign as kings.

Go now with me to Jeremiah, 23d chapter, and let us read the 5th and 6th verses.

"Behold, the days come, saith the Lord, that I will raise unto David a righteous Branch, and a King shall reign and prosper, and shall execute judgment and justice in the earth. In his days Judah shall be saved, and Israel shall dwell safely: and this is the name whereby he shall be called, THE LORD OUR RIGHTEOUSNESS."

Remember, if you please, the name of the King here spoken of. He is to be called THE LORD OUR RIGHTEOUSNESS. He is called, also, a Righteous Branch, and the Kind who should reign and prosper.

Go with me now to Jeremiah, 33d chapter and 15th verse, and, or including the 18th.

"In those days, and at that time, will I cause the Branch of righteousness to grow up unto David; and he shall execute judgment and righteousness in the land. In those days shall Judah be saved, and Jerusalem shall dwell safely: and this is the name wherewith he shall be called, The Lord our righteousness. For thus saith the Lord; David shall never want a man to sit upon the throne of the house of Israel; neither shall the priests the Levites, want a man before me to offer burnt offerings, and to kindle meat offerings, and to do sacrifice continually."

Again, at the 19th verse we are told "The word of the Lord came," &c.

"And the word of the Lord came to Jeremiah, saying, Thus saith the Lord; If ye can break my covenant of the day, and my covenant of the night, and that there should not be day and night in their season; then may also my covenant be broken with David, my servant, that he should not have a son to reign upon his throne; and with the Levites, the priests, my ministers."

Again, at the 25th verse of this same chapter, and on to the end, we are told: "Thus saith the Lord; If my covenant be not with day and night, and if I have not apointed the ordinances of heaven and earth; then will I cast away the seed of Jacob, and David my servant, so that I will not take any of his seed to be rulers over the seed of Abraham, Isaac and Jacob: for I will cause their captivity to return, and have mercy on them."

Here are presented two or three thoughts which I wish to examine with care. In the first place, in the 20th and 21st verses, the Lord declares:

"Thus saith the Lord; If ye can break my covenant of the day, and my covenant of the night, and that there should not be day and night in their season; then may also my covenant be broken with David, my servant, that he should not have a son to reign upon his throne; and with the Levites, the priests, my ministers.".

Let us ask the question just here, has there ever a period of time passed, from the days of Jeremiah down to the present time, when there was not day and night? and while 1 ask that question, mark the manner in which it is emphatically repeated in the 25th and 26th verses:

"Thus saith the Lord; If my covenant be not with day and night, and if I have not appointed the ordinances of heaven and earth; then will I cast away the seed of Jacob, and David my servant, so that I will not take any of his seed to be rulers over the seed of Abraham, Isaac and Jacob: for I will cause their captivity to return, and have mercy on them."

Pause for a moment and examine the matter before us. We have here confirmed in the most positive manner possible, the thought that David should never want a man to sit on the throne of his kingdom. The illustration here used to impress this thought is borrowed from the very laws that control the physical world around us—that govern the earth on which we live. We are told that David shall never want a man to sit on his throne so long as those immutable laws of nature hold their sway. It so happens, however, that we find, that the last of the lineal descendants of king David was found upon the Hebrew throne at Jerusalem when our Savior was upon earth; and hence, if the Messiah himself has not been upon the throne from the time when he ascended up into heaven to this very hour, then there has been this long interim in which there was no one on the throne of David.

Go with me now to Zechariah 6th chapter, 12th and 13th verses:

"And speak unto him, saying, Thus speaketh the Lord of hosts, saying, Behold the man whose name is The BRANCH; and he shall grow up out of his place, and he shall build the temple of the Lord: Even he shall build the temple of the Lord; and he shall bear the glory, and shall sit and rule upon his throne; and he shall be a priest upon his throne: and the counsel of peace shall be between them both."

One thought which I wish to fasten just here is this: The Messiah, who is indisputably the being here spoken of, is to be "a priest *upon* his throne." He must either be a priest now or not. If he is not now a priest, then there is now no high priest—and if there is now no high priest before the Lord, then there is now no possible medium through which man can find access to the throne of God and the black wings of everlasting despair are brooding over all creation. He is to be a priest *on his throne*. Mark that the text does not say *on* and *off* his throne—but it says *on* his throne. It does not say either, that he shall be a priest on the throne of another, but on *his* throne—his own throne. If he is now on his throne, then, as a natural consequence, as none but kings are on their thrones, he is now king: and if he is now king—he is now king and priest, and if king and priest then is he king and priest forever, after the order of Melchisedec. Mark the manner in which they are conjoined together. I repeat the declaration, that just so sure as he is a priest now, just so sure is he a king now, and there is not a hint from the first word in Genesis to the last amen in Revelations, concerning his being a priest anywhere but "on his throne."

We pause here one moment to call your attention to Zechariah 9th chapter and 9th verse:

"Rejoice greatly, O daughter of Zion; shout, O daughter of Jerusalem; behold, thy King cometh unto thee: he is just, and having salvation; lowly, and riding upon an ass, and upon a colt the foal of an ass."

Mark the force of the word "cometh"—He comes—He is approaching. Look now at John's Gospel, 12th chapter, 12th, 13th, 14th and 15th verses. You will there find that when the Savior was riding in triumph to Jerusalem, the multitude were crying, "Hosannah to the Son of David." This prophecy, found in Zechariah, was then fulfilled. The King was coming unto Jerusalem, "just and having salvation, lowly and riding upon an ass." But he could not be a priest upon his throne upon this earth, and therefore it was necessary that he should pass away from earth. Go with me now to the Acts of the Apostles, 1st chapter, and 9th verse: "And when he had spoken these things while they beheld, he was taken up; and a cloud received him out of their sight." In connection with this thought, turn your attention to Acts, 2d chapter, 29th and 36th verses, inclusive:

"Men and brethren, let me freely speak unto you of the patriarch David that he is both dead and buried, and his sepulchre is with us unto this day. Therefore being a prophet, and knowing that God had sworn with an oath to him, that of the fruit of his loins, according to the flesh, he would raise up Christ to sit on his throne; He, seeing this before, spake of the resurrection of Christ, that his soul was not left in hell, neither his flesh did see corruption. This Jesus hath God raised up, whereof we all are witnesses. Therefore being by the right hand of God exalted, and having received of the Father the promise of the Holy Ghost, he hath shed forth this, which ye now see and hear. For David is not ascended into the heavens: but he saith himself, The Lord said unto my Lord, Sit thou on my right hand, until I make thy foes thy footstool. Therefore let all the house of Israel know assuredly, that God hath made that same Jesus, whom ye have crucified, both Lord and Christ."

Let us pause here for one moment. We find here a quotation from the 110th Psalm and 1st verse, where the Father is represented as saying to the Son, "Sit thou on my right hand until I make thy foes thy footstool." This is spoken of by the voice of revelation as taking place when the Son of the Highest ascended on high. This same passage is quoted six or seven times in the New Testament writings. Here, at the right hand of the Father the Son was to sit until his enemies were all subdued and put under his feet. But Paul, in his first letter to the Corinthians, 15th chapter and 26th verse, demonstrates that one of those enemies is Death. In the 25th verse of the same chapter we learn that he must "reign until he hath put all things under his feet." "The last enemy that shall be destroyed is Death." Now, Death cannot be destroyed until all ruling power is taken from him. All ruling power cannot be taken from him while he has control over one solitary human being. Consequently, the Son is to remain at his Father's right hand till the very last human being shall be brought out of Death's dominions. This being so, what becomes of the thought of his coming down to this earth and setting up an earthly throne, and reigning here a thousand years? You and I know very well that all ruling power cannot be taken from Death until the last human being is brought out from under Death's dominion. As long as one soiltary human being remains subject to Death, Death will still possess ruling power, and as Death cannot be put under his feet until all ruling power is taken from Death, the Son must remain at the Father's right hand until after the final resurrection and the final consummation of all things.

We are now prepared to look upon the coronation scene of the king. You recollect that in the first chapter of the Acts of the Apostles we are told that he ascended into heaven and a cloud received him out of their sight. The Psalmist in the 24th Psalm gives us a description of the coronation scenes. As the king with his angelic escort approaches the gates of the city the cry is heard, "Lift up your heads, O ye gates, and be ye lift up ye everlasting doors, and the king of glory shall come in." The demand from within the portals is heard. "Who is this King of Glory?" The response to this demand from the approaching host is, "The Lord strong and mighty; the Lord mighty in battle." The allusion here is to his recent victory over death. Once more the demand is made, "Lift up your heads, O ye gates and the king of glory shall come in!" The gates fly open wide and the Son passes into the city through the portals of eternal day.

Go now to Daniel 7th chapter, 13th and 14th verses. "I saw in the night visions, and behold, one like the Son of man came with the clouds of heaven, and came to the

Ancient of days, and they brought him near before him. And there was given him dominion, and glory and a kingdom, that all people, nations, and languages, should serve him; his dominion is an everlasting dominion, which shall not pass away, and his kingdom, that which shall not be destroyed."

The escort brought the Son near, before the throne of the Father, and then, at that time there was given unto him "dominion and glory and a kingdom," and so on. Here Daniel beholds the glories of the coronation scene. John the Revelator speaks of the Son as being crowned. Then Daniel, standing on the other side, before the coronation, sees him in prophetic vision brought near to the ancient of days, who is on the eternal throne, and there beholds him crowned and invested with dominion and glory and a kingdom. Just so, John the Revelator, standing upon this side of the coronation, and looking backward at the same scene says: "And I saw heaven opened, and behold a white horse; and he that sat upon him was called Faithful and True, and in righteousness he doth judge and make war. His eyes were as a flame of fire, and on his head were many crowns; and he had a name written, that no man knew, but he himself. And he was clothed with a vesture dipped in blood; and his name is called The Word of God. And the armies which were in heaven followed him upon white horses, clothed in fine linen, white and clean. And out of his mouth goeth a sharp sword, that with it he should smite the nations; and he shall rule them with a rod of iron; and he treadeth the winepress of the fierceness and wrath of Almighty God. [And he hath on his vesture, and on his thigh a name was written, KING OF KINGS, AND LORD OF LORDS."

Here John speaks of the same personage described by Daniel. He wears a vesture dipped in blood and upon his vesture and upon his thigh there is a name written KING OF KINGS, AND LORD OF LORDS. In heaven the Son of God wears this title. That is where Daniel saw him, and where John saw him. In our next we shall be prepreparced to examine the question of the issuing of laws.

## NEG.—J. M. STEPHENSON—SECOND SPEECH.

I call your attention to one of the objections made by my opponent to the position I took in my first speech. I am represented as taking the position that Adam lost the dominion in the sense of having actually possessed it. The position I took is that he was *offered* that dominion upon certain conditions; that he failed to comply with those conditions, and therefore failed to receive the dominion which he would have had in case of obedience; and that in this sense, not in the other, he *lost* it. The second Adam complied with the conditions, and he will yet receive the dominion, at his second advent, when he sits on the throne of his glory. This is my position correctly stated.

What would have been the duration of Adam's probation had he been obedient to the law of God, is not named in the Holy Scriptures. For my opponent to affirm that he would have entered upon the reward immediately is to beg the whole question. Where Revelation is silent it is not the right of any man to say what God's purposes were, or to pretend to reveal the secret counsels of the Most High.

I call your attention to the subject before us, just where I left it. I had just affirmed that the covenant God made with Abraham, He also promised to make with Abraham and Christ, and all that were Christ's. Turn now to Romans, 4th chapter, and 13th verse. "For the promise, that he should be the heir of the world, was not to Abraham, or to his seed, through the law, but through the righteousness of faith."

Here you find a promise made to Abraham and to his seed. I have proved already that the seed referred to here was Christ himself and also all who are Christ's. They are to be the world's possessor's when heirship shall have been merged into possession.

Again, God selected David from among his brethren, and allied him with a kingdom on earth which he denominated *his* kingdom, and which when restored will be his everlasting kingdom—one kingdom and not two separate and distinct kingdoms. A kingdom restored is the same kingdom after the restoration that it was before. If the kingdom of Great Britain should be overthrown and afterward restored, it would be the kingdom of Great Britain still as truly as though it had never been subverted. Just so, when the kingdom shall be RESTORED to the house of David, and when Christ shall sit upon HIS throne, that kingdom will be as truly the kingdom of David, and his throne, as truly David's throne, as though there had never been an interregnum in the kingly line. The fact that for the time being there is no one upon David's throne, does not prove that God has two kingdoms or ever will have two kingdoms upon earth. I wish now to investigate the relation of King David to the throne, as God's representative. That the throne of David and the kingdom over which he reigned, were the throne and kingdom of God" will be amply proven and demonstrated in the further development of this subject. And that God has promised and pledged his word to perpetuate David's kingdom through "David's Son" and the "Son of God," I will proceed to prove.

Before I proceed further, however, I wish to call your attention to two essential elements of a kingdom—first a kingdom must have a king and subjects, and that in this respect the kingdom of God will not be an exception to other kingdoms. I shall prove to you that Jesus Christ, the son of David and the Son of God, will be the king who shall reign over the kingdom of God forever and over, and that the twelve tribes of Israel will be the subjects over whom he shall reign. My first proof is drawn from 2d Samuel, 7th chapter, commencing at the 12th verse.

"And when thy days be fulfilled, and thou shalt sleep with thy fathers, I will set up thy seed after thee, which shall proceed out of thy bowels, and I will establish his kingdom. He shall build a house for my name, and I will establish the throne of his kingdom forever. I will be his father, and he shall be my son. If he commit iniquity, I will chasten him with the rod of men, and with the stripes of the children of men. But my mercy shall not depart away from him, as I took it from Saul, whom I put away before thee. And thy house and thy kingdom shall be established forever before thee; thy throne shall be established forever. According to all these words, and according to all this vision, so did Nathan speak unto David. Then went king David in, and sat before the Lord, and he said, Who am I, O Lord God? and what is my house, that thou hast brought me hitherto? And this was yet a small thing in thy sight, O Lord God; but thou hast spoken also of thy servant's house for a great while to come. And is this the manner of man, O Lord God?"

You will find the same promise and covenant alluded to in 1 Chronicles, 17th chapter, from the 11th to the 15th verses inclusive. "And it shall come to pass, when thy days be expired that thou must go to be with thy fathers, that I will raise up thy seed after thee, which shall be of thy sons; and I will establish his kingdom. He shall build me a house, and I will establish his throne forever. I will be his father, and he shall be my son: and I will not take my mercy away from him, as I took it from *him* that was before thee. But I will settle him in mine house and in my kingdom forever; and his throne shall be established for evermore. According to all these words, and according to all this vision, so did Nathan speak unto David."

I wish to call your attention to the fact, that the son of David spoken of in the 7th chapter of 2d Samuel, who should build a house for the name of the Lord, and the throne of whose kingdom should be established forever and ever is CHRIST himself. It is urged that this promise relates to Solomon, from the fact it is promised that this son of David is to build the house of the Lord. Solomon built the house of the Lord, and therefore it is claimed that it was in him that this promise was to be fulfilled. I would observe in the first place that all the promises of

God in relation to this personage, here spoken of must centre in some ONE person. It is not enough for some of the promises to centre in ONE individual while others do not. All must point to ONE person and meet their fulfillment in him. The word of the Lord must stand forever. Inspiration never yet made a mistake—hence the person through whom the kingdom shall be established forever must be one in whom every promise made by God through the prophet to David shall find its complete fulfillment. Turn to the 2d chapter of 1st Kings and read from the 1st to the 4th verse inclusive. Listen to the dying charge of David to his son Solomon:

"Now the days of David drew nigh that he should die; and he charged Solomon his son, saying, I go the way of all the earth: be thou strong therefore, and show thyself a man; and keep the charge of the Lord thy God, to walk in his ways, to keep his statutes, and his commandments, and his judgments, and his testimonies, as it is written in the law of Moses, that thou mayest prosper in all tha thou doest, and whithersoever thou turnest thyself: that the Lord may continue his word which he spake concerning me, saying, If thy children take heed to their way, to walk before me in truth with all their heart and with all their soul, there shall not fail thee, said he, a man on the throne of Israel."

Turn now to the 132d Psalm, and you will there find a conditional promise made to David's seed. You can not fail to notice that the promise contained in the 7th chap. of 2d Sam., has no conditions annexed to it. There God says he *will* establish the throne of David forever and ever. There is no condition, nor contingency named in this prophecy upon which the fulfillment of this promise can possibly be forfeited. Here we see the two sons of David, Solomon and Christ, placed in strong and direct contrast with each other. So far as Christ is concerned, there is no condition whatever connected with the promise, but so far as Solomon and his successors were concerned, there were conditions specified, upon which their throne and dominion should be perpetuated. Let me read the language contained in the 132d Psalm, 11th and 12th verses. I believe the Holy Spirit understands the use of language, and can use words which will most clearly and correctly represent to our minds the Spirit's ideas.

"The Lord hath sworn in truth unto David; he will not turn from it; of the fruit of thy body will I set upon thy throne. If thy children will keep my covenant and my testimony that I shall teach them, their children shall also sit upon thy throne for evermore."

I will now prove to you that the first successors of David failed to comply with the conditions annexed to the promise, and forfeited the promised privilege. Listen to the language of the inspired historian, recorded in the 1 Kings, 11th chapter, 6th to the 11th verses inclusively:

"And Solomon did evil in the sight of the Lord, and went not fully after the Lord, as did David his father. Then did Solomon build a high place for Chemosh, the abomination of Moab, in the hill that is before Jerusalem, and for Molech, the abomination of the children of Ammon. And likewise did he for all his strange wives, which burnt incense and sacrificed unto their gods. And the Lord was angry with Solomon, because his heart was turned from the Lord God of Israel, which had appeared unto him twice, and had commanded him concerning this thing, that he should not go after other gods: but he kept not that which the Lord commanded. Wherefore the Lord said unto Solomon, Forasmuch as this is done of thee, and thou hast not kept my covenant and my statutes, which I have commanded thee, I will surely rend the kingdom from thee, and will give it to thy servant."

Also, chapter 12: 20–24:

"And it came to pass, when all Israel heard that Jeroboam was come again, that they sent and called him unto the congregation, and made him king over all Israel: there was none that followed the house of David, but the tribe of Judah only. And when Rehoboam was come to Jerusalem, he assembled all the house of Judah, with the tribe of Benjamin, a hundred and fourscore thousand chosen men, which were warriors, to fight against the house of Israel, to bring the kingdom again to Rehoboam the son of Solomon. But the word of God came unto Shemaiah the man of God, saying, Speak unto Rehoboam the son of Solomon, king of Judah, and unto all the house of Judah and Benjamin, and to the remnant of the people, saying, Thus saith the Lord, Ye shall not go up, nor fight against your brethren the children of Israel: return every man to his house; for this thing is from me. They hearkened therefore to the word of the Lord and returned to depart, according to the word of the Lord."

Hence you see the right of David's having a perpetual representative on his throne was suspended on condition of obedience: Solomon failed to comply with the conditions, and the kingdom was taken from him and given to his servant. His kingdom was broken up. Two tribes only remained for a time attached to the throne of David; then those two were scattered to the four winds of heaven, and during eighteen hundred years David has had no royal representative upon his throne and kingdom.

Now, in reference to Solomon's building the Temple of the Lord; go with me to Zechariah. My opponent may affirm as often as he pleases that we have no King unless Christ is now a King. Let us turn from his assertions and read the glorious promise made by God through his prophet. It is found in Zechariah, 6th chapter, 12th and 13th verses:

"And speak unto him, saying, Thus speaketh the Lord of hosts, saying, Behold the man whose name is The BRANCH; and he shall grow up out of his place, and he shall build the temple of the Lord: even he shall build the temple of the Lord; and he shall bear the glory, and shall sit and rule upon his throne; and he shall be a priest upon his throne; and the counsel of peace shall be between them both."

I did not emphasize the pronoun "he" in this passage, as I should have done. We can not emphasize God's truth—the sacred promises on which he has hinged his future and everlasting Kingdom too strongly. I will read the passage again:

"And speak unto him, saying, Thus speaketh the Lord of hosts, saying, Behold the man whose name is The BRANCH; and he shall grow up out of his place, and he shall build the temple of the Lord: even he shall build the temple of the Lord; and he shall bear the glory, and shall sit and rule upon his throne; and he shall be a priest upon his throne: and the counsel of peace shall be between them both."

Now, as to whether this throne is beyond or below the heavens—whether it is to be set up on the earth or far beyond the feeblest and most distant star that glitters in the pathway of heaven. I call your attention to the 33d chapter of Jeremiah. I wonder that my opponent did not blush when the assertion was read that he should rule "on the land." I wish to prove that this "Righteous Branch" here spoken of by Jeremiah is none other than God's vicegerent upon earth, the Lord Jesus Christ, and that his throne will be set up here on the earth, and not above the starry heavens. It is one thing simply to read over the words of testimony, and it is quite another to read the language and emphasize it properly, according to its true sense, and according to the meaning contained in it. Listen, if you please, to the prophet Jeremiah in the 33d chapter of his prophecy, commencing at the 15th and to the 19th, inclusively:

"In those days, and at that time, will I cause the Branch of righteousness to grow up unto David; and he shall execute judgment and righteousness in the land. In those days shall Judah be saved, and Jerusalem shall dwell safely: and this is the name wherewith he shall be called, The Lord our Righteousness. For thus saith the Lord: David shall never want a man to sit upon the throne of the house of Israel; neither shall the priests the Levites want a man before me to offer burnt-offerings, and to kindle meat-offerings, and to do sacrifice continually."

Jesus Christ shall then be a kingly priest upon his throne—he shall build the temple of the Lord—he shall execute judgment and righteousness in the land—and he shall be called, The Lord our Righteousness.

From what point of time forward is it that David shall never want a man to sit upon his throne? I answer, from the time when the throne of Israel is established and Judah gathered home, and when the righteous King shall begin to execute judgment and righteousness "in the land."

"For thus saith the Lord: David shall never want a man to sit upon the throne of the house of Israel; neither shall the priests the Levites want a man before me to offer burnt-offerings, and to kindle meat-offerings, and to do sacrifice continually."

Will my opponent attempt to break the covenant of the Almighty God, which pledges him to bind Christ to David's throne so that David shall nevermore want a man to sit on his throne? If he does I would forewarn him of the mighty task before him. The Lord says, that unless you can break his covenant of the day and of the night you cannot break the covenant he has made that David's seed should inherit the throne of his kingdom forever and ever. Read the 20th and 21st verses of the 33d chapter of Jeremiah, my friend, and see what your prospect is of accomplishing the task you have taken upon yourself:

"Thus saith the Lord; If ye can break my covenant of the day, and my covenant of the night, and that there should not be day and night in their season; Then may also my covenant be broken with David my servant, that he should not have a son to reign upon his throne; and with the Levites the priests, my ministers."

I would advise you to read the 24th, 25th and 26th verses of the same chapter:

"Considerest thou not what this people have spoken, saying, The two families which the Lord hath chosen, he hath even cast them off? thus they have despised my people, that they should be no more a nation before them. Thus saith the Lord; If my covenant be not with day and night, and if I have not appointed the ordinances of heaven and earth; then will I cast away the seed of Jacob and David my servant, so that I will not take any of his seed to be rulers over the seed of Abraham, Isaac, and Jacob: for I will cause their captivity to return, and have mercy on them."

I am afraid my friend Russell is implicated here. If he and his friends take away the promises which God has made to Israel, and apply those promises to a Gentile church, would it not be to stamp them with an everlasting stigma? It would prove to an intelligent creation that you despise God's people, and covenant.

From this time forward, we are told that David shall never want a man to sit upon his throne, and from that time forward this Righteous Branch, spoken of by the prophet, instead of being seated upon a throne in heaven, is to reign as a king upon earth, and his subjects are to be the twelve tribes of Israel.

## AFF.—P. T. RUSSELL—THIRD SPEECH.

At the conclusion of my last speech we had just ascertained the time of the coronation of the King. Having found that the time of the coronation of the King was the time of his ascension on high, I was just on the point of bringing to your minds the thrilling contrast that there is between the coming spoken of by the prophet Daniel, and that which shall be when he comes to revisit our earth. In the 13th verse of the 2d chapter of Titus we have these words: "Looking for that blessed hope, and the glorious appearing of the great God and our Savior Jesus Christ."

Here the Father and the Son are spoken of as coming together. It is called the glorious appearing of the great God and our Savior Jesus Christ. On the other hand let us call your attention to the language employed by Daniel, when speaking of the time when universal empire was to be given to the Son.

"I saw in the night visions, and behold, *one* like the Son of man came with the clouds of heaven, and came to the Ancient of Days, and they brought him near before him. And there was given him dominion, and glory, and a kingdom, that all people, nations and languages should serve him; his dominion is an everlasting dominion, which shall not pass away, and his kingdom *that* which shall not be destroyed."

Here we have a thrilling contrast. When the Son shall come again to judge the quick and the dead, he shall come *with* his Father. When he came to the place where he was to receive the grant of universal empire he came to the Ancient of Days—he came to the Father and we are told that then, when he was escorted by the multitude of the celestial host near to the Father's throne, then there was given unto him a kingdom, that all people, nations and languages should serve him. You will find the language of the Apostle in Hebrews, 1st Chapter, 8th and 9th verses in perfect keeping and harmony with the view here presented. He then represents the Father as saying to the Son:

"Thy throne, O God, *is* for ever and ever; a sceptre of righteousness *is* the sceptre of thy kingdom. Thou hast loved righteousness, and hated iniquity; therefore God, *even* thy God, hath annointed thee with the oil of gladness above thy fellows."

While thus we have before us the fact that the time of the ceronation of the King as Lord of all, was at the time of his ascension into heaven. Keep also before your minds in connection with this thought the simple truth, that when the Son had thus ascended on high, had been thus crowned Lord of all, and was thus seated at the right hand of the Father he was to remain there until all his foes should be subdued. Now one of the foes that should be subdued is death; consequently the Son must remain seated at the right hand of the Father until the last human being shall have been brought out from under death's dominion, or in other words until the final resurrection.

We here leave this point in order to speak of the issuing of laws. Turn if you please to Micah, 4th Chapter, 1st and 2d verses:

"But in the last days it shall come to pass, *that* the mountain of the house of the Lord shall be established in the top of the mountains, and it shall be exalted above the hills; and people shall flow unto it. And many nations shall come and say, Come, and let us go up to the mountain of the Lord, and to the house of the God of Jacob; and he will teach us of his ways, and we will walk in his paths: for the law shall go forth of Zion, and the word of the Lord from Jerusalem."

This law of the King was to go forth at that point of time called "last days." In the preceding chapter it is declared that "Zion shall be ploughed as a field, and Jerusalem shall become heaps, and the mountain of the house as the high places of the forest." This is a vivid description of the overthrow and demolition of the city of Jerusalem, and then follows a prophetic declaration of what shall come to pass "in the last days,"—that is to say, the last days of the city of Jerusalem immediately before the demolition and overthrow that had just been described. "In the last days it shall come to pass that the mountain of the Lord's house shall be established in the top of the mountains, and shall be exalted above the hills, and people shall flow unto it."

In perfect harmony with this is the language of inspiration in Acts, 2d Chapter, 16th and 17th verses. When upon the day of Pentecost, the Holy Ghost was poured out upon the disciples, and they began to speak with other tongues as the Spirit gave them utterance, the multitude came together inquiring what caused that very unusual phenomenon. Peter in answer to their questions says:

"But this is that which was spoken by the prophet Joel; and it shall come to pass in the last days, saith God, I will pour out of my Spirit upon all flesh: and your sons and your daughters shall prophesy, and your young men shall see visions, and your old men shall dream dreams."

Mark the peculiar force of the words, "last days." Observe that the voice of inspiration here declares that the very things that were being seen and heard there in the city of Jerusalem were the identical events foretold by the prophet, and that should come to pass in these "last days." Here we have clearly presented to our minds the idea of the time when these last days should occur. This being on the day of Pentecost, we have fixed the time when Micah said the law should go forth of Zion, and the word of the Lord from Jerusalem. "This," said Peter, calling their attention to what was right before the eyes of his hearers; "this that you now see" is the idea; "this" is that which was spoken of by the prophet Joel, and which he said should take place in these last days. Now, either that point of time called "last days" by the prophet had come when Peter lived, or it had not; if it had not come, then the prophecy itself is all out of joint; but we cannot believe that prophecy is out of joint, and the inevitable consequence is that all who believe God's truth must come to the conclusion that the time designated by the prophet as "last days," had come in the time of Peter, and that the prophecy was fulfilled upon the day of Pentecost.

Let us turn now, and examine the 110th Psalm, and see how this matter stands before us. Read the language contained in the 1st and 2d verses:

"The Lord said unto my Lord, Sit thou at my right hand, until I make thine enemies thy footstool. The Lord shall send the rod of thy strength out of Zion: rule thou in the midst of thine enemies."

"Rule thou in the midst of thine enemies." Where? "*In the midst of thine enemies.*" Listen to the remaining verses of this Psalm:

"Thy people shall be willing in the day of thy power, in the beauties of holiness from the womb of the morning: thou hast the dew of thy youth. The Lord hath sworn, and will not repent. Thou at a priest forever after the order of Melchizedek. The Lord at thy right hand shall strike through kings in the day of his wrath. He shall judge among the heathen, he shall fill the places with the dead bodies; he shall wound the heads over many countries. He shall drink of the brook in the way: therefore shall he lift up the head."

Observe now, if you please, that all this is referred to the time of the Savior's ruling—when he should rule in the midst of his enemies—when the Lord of Hosts in his wrath should strike through kings—when the dead bodies of his enemies should lie scattered about over the face of the country. And this was to be at the very time when he was to be a priest forever after the order of Melchizedek. This brings us back again to the time when the law should go forth of Zion, and the word of the Lord from Jerusalem. From this point it stretches on and on, without a single break of one moment until the time when the last human being shall be brought out of Death's dominion. "The last enemy that shall be destroyed is death." Death never can be destroyed so long as death has ruling power; but death will have ruling power as long as one human being remains under his dominion; and hence the conclusion is irresistible that the Son is to remain at the Father's right hand until all the family of man that have been in their graves shall come forth, forever free from the power and dominion of the "grim monster." And if the Son remains at the right hand of the Father until that time, I am perfectly sure of one thing, and that is this: that ever since the time when the Righteous Branch, spoken of by the prophet, was raised up, even down to this present hour, he has been sitting upon his throne enjoying the possession of the Kingdom spoken of in Daniel, 2d chapter and 44th verse.

I now invite your careful attention to the next point which presents itself for our consideration, which is one of the requirements or essential elements of a Kingdom: subjects, submitting themselves to be governed by the laws. And again I call your attention to the language of Micah, 4th chapter and 2d verse. It is there not only stated that the law should go forth from Zion and the word of the Lord from Jerusalem, but is is also asserted that "many nations shall come and say, Come, and let us go up to the mountain of the LORD, and to the house of the God of Jacob, and he will teach us of his ways, and we will walk in his paths." The first thought that I wish to impress upon your minds just here, is the idea of the "many nations" here mentioned. Go, now, with me to the Acts of the Apostles, and let us read from the 2d chapter, beginning with the 2d verse:

"And suddenly there came a sound from heaven as of a mighty rushing wind, and it filled all the house where they were sitting. And there appeared unto them cloven tongues like as of fire, and it sat upon each of them. And they were all filled with the Holy Ghost, and began to speak with other tongues, as the Spirit gave them utterance. And there were dwelling at Jerusalem Jews, devout men, out of every nation under heaven. Now when this was noised abroad, the multitude came together, and were confounded, because that every man heard them speak in his own language. And they were all amazed and marvelled, saying one to another, Behold, are not all these which speak Galileans? And how hear we every man in our own tongue, wherein we were born? Parthians, and Medes, and Elamites, and the dwellers in Mesopotamia, and in Judea, and Cappadocia, in Pontas and Asia, Phyrgia, and Pamphylia, in Egypt, and in the parts of Libya about Cyrene, and strangers of Rome, Jews and proselytes, Cretes and Arabians, we do hear them speak in our tongues the wonderful works of God."

Here we have multitudes coming together, and for what purpose? Micah answers the question beforehand. The multitudes were to say, "Come and let us go up to the house of the God of Jacob; he will teach us of his ways, and we will walk in his paths." The purpose of their coming was to learn the ways of the Lord, that they might walk in his paths, because out of Mount Zion should go forth the law, and the word of the Lord from Jerusalem. Having made this inquiry, and finding it thus answered, let us listen further to the language of Peter on this important occasion. Christ had been crucified—

he had been buried—he had risen again from the dead, and ascended up on high; and this is the grand turning point of the apostle's theme. In the 36th verse, in evident allusion to the exaltation of Christ to the right hand of the Father on high, he says to them:

"Therefore let all the house of Israel know that God hath made that same Jesus whom ye have crucified, both Lord and Christ." And we are told in the following verse, that when they heard this they were pierced to the heart, and said, "Men and brethren, what shall we do?" Here was a call for a royal law; they were at that very time standing upon Mount Zion, the mountain of the city of Jerusalem upon which the temple stood. Here were multitudes of people from many nations, gathered together unto the house of the Lord. They called for the law that should go forth from Mount Zion, and it was given them in these words, found in the 38th and 39th verses:

"Then Peter said unto them, Repent, and be baptized every one of you in the name of Jesus Christ for the remission of sins, and ye shall receive the gift of the Holy Ghost. For the promise is unto you, and to your children, and to all that are afar off, even as many as the Lord our God shall call."

Here we have the law issued from Mount Zion and the word of the Lord going forth from Jerusalem; and in close connection therewith we find subjects by the thousand submitting to that law. In the 41st verse of the same chapter we read:

"Then they that gladly received his word were baptized: and the same day there were added unto them about three thousand souls."

Here we have found already all of the essential elements of a kingdom: first a King, crowned; second, the issuing of laws; third, subjects submitting to those laws. They all concentrate upon the day mentioned in Acts, 2d chapter and first verse: "And when the day of Pentecost was fully come, they were all with one accord in one place." Here, then, we might with perfect confidence forever rest the argument, and assert that the Kingdom of God was set up on the day of Pentecost.

Here, however, are other matters of moment to which I call your attention. Paul, in the epistle to the Corinthians, 1st chapter and 13th verse, in allusion to the Father, says:

"Who hath delivered us from the power of darkness, and translated us into the kingdom of his dear son."

Now, mark that the kingdom here spoken of is called by the apostle, "the kingdom of God's dear Son." Mark, in connection with this thought, another fact, that Paul and his brethren, according to his own statement, were at that time already translated into that kingdom. In the 12th chapter of Hebrews, and at the 28th verse, the apostle speaking of this same kingdom, says, that he and his brethren were then receiving it: "Wherefore we, rereceiving a kingdom which cannot be moved, let us have grace whereby we may serve God acceptably with reverence and godly fear." They were receiving it, and it was a kingdom which could not be moved. Daniel, 2d chapter and 44th verse, has precisely the same idea expressed in these words, that the kingdom is one that "shall never be destroyed." The words in both places indicate exactly the same thing. In Daniel it is said not only that the kingdom shall not be destroyed, but also, that it "shall not be left to other people." In the other place, Hebrews, 12th chapter, 28th verse, it is said that Paul and his brethren were then receiving it. In Daniel, 7th chapter and 18th verse, it is said, "the saints of the Most High shall take the kingdom and possess the kingdom forever, even forever and ever." The term "take" used here, is a military term. They were to *take* the kingdom and possess it forever and forever. While this is the length of the period in which the kingdom should be possessed, observe that in the other place, Daniel, 2d chapter, 44th verse, it is said that "the kingdom shall not be left to other people." Here, too, we find an explanation of the peculiar language of the apostle John in Revelations, 1st chapter and 9th verse:

"I, John, who am also your brother, and companion in tribulation, and in the kingdom and patience of Jesus Christ, was in the isle that is called Patmos, for the word of God, and for the testimony of Jesus Christ."

Here John not only represents himself as being with his brethren in tribulation, but also in the kingdom of our Lord and Savior Jesus Christ. That kingdom must have been in existence then or John could not have been in it as he says he was. That kingdom also must have been in existence at the time when Paul wrote his Colossian letter, for, if it was not, he could not have told the truth when he said he and his brethren had been translated into it. Neither the declaration of John the revelator, nor that of the Apostle Paul could be reconciled with truth upon any other hypothesis than this—that the kingdom of God was already set up; and here again we might with perfect safety rest the argument.

Go with me to Matthew, 3d chapter and 1st and 2d verses: "In those days came John the Baptist, preaching in the wilderness of Judea, and saying, Repent ye, for the kingdom of heaven is at hand." What does the language of the second verse mean? It can not be construed to mean anything more or less than this: that the kingdom of heaven was near by—that it was come nigh unto them. The Savior after he was baptized, said: "Repent, for the kingdom of heaven is at hand." He sent out his seventy disciples to tell the people the kingdom of heaven is at hand; repent, and believe, and be baptized. Our Savior taught his disciples, when they prayed, to say: "Our Father, who art in heaven, hallowed be thy name; *thy kingdom come.*" All these circumstances indicate clearly and conclusively the fact that the kingdom of God had not yet come, but was near at hand. But let us go a little farther. The enemies of Christ have put him to death. He enters Death's domain; but on the third day he rises from the tomb. After his resurrection from the grave, we see him standing upon the earth surrounded by his disciples. He lifts his hands and bestows upon them his last parting blessing. He then ascends in their view, until a bright cloud receives him out of their sight. And as he ascends the skies, attended by his angelic escort, the voice of the Father is heard saying unto him: "Because thou hast loved righteousness and hated iniquity, sit thou on my right hand until I make thy foes thy footstool." While we have this testimony upon one side in point of time of the death, resurrection, and ascension of the Savior, on the other side of that event in point of time, we have evidence no less strong by which to establish the fact that the kingdom of God was set up at the time already indicated. Before the period of Christ's resurrection from the dead and his ascending upon high, the kingdom of God is uniformly spoken of as being at hand; while on the other hand, after that event, no one, by God's authority, speaks of it as being at hand, but all the inspired writers speak of it as being already established. People were said to have been translated into that kingdom, and as having received it.

Our next point will be the increase or growth of this kingdom; for, mark you, if the kingdom of God is not to be set up until the end of all things shall come, then that kingdom can never know any such thing as increase.

## NEG.—J. M. STEPHENSON—THIRD SPEECH.

I have nothing to which to reply in the present argument. I will simply employ the language of John: "Prepare ye the way of the Lord." Every mountain of objection shall be laid low; the crooked places shall be made straight and the rough places smooth; that the car of truth may move on majestically and gloriously. I shall notice only such objections as are thrown across the track of God's eternal truth. I desire, in the first place, to read to you the last words the sweet psalmist of Israel ever uttered. You remember the covenant God made with David, concerning his throne and kingdom, as recorded in the 7th chapter of 2d Samuel, and in the 17th chapter of 2d Chronicles. You recollect that when my time expired I had just introduced the eternal Jehovah as a witness. Now I desire that David may be brought in as a witness, in order to prepare the way for the great Jehovah, in reference to the nature of the covenant which God made with him just before his death. The language to which I refer you may find in 2d Samuel, 23d chapter. I will read the first five verses: "Now, these be the last words of David. David, the son of Jesse, said, and the man who was raised up on high, the annointed of the God of Jacob, and the sweet psalmist of Israel, said: The Spirit of the Lord spake by me, and his word was in my tongue. The God of Israel said, the Rock of Israel spake to me, He that ruleth over men must be just, ruling in the fear of God. And he shall be as the light of the morning when the sun riseth, even a morning without clouds: as the tender grass springing out of the earth by clear shining after rain. Although my house be not so with God; yet he hath made with me an everlasting covenant, ordered in all things, and sure: for this is all my salvation and all my desire, although he make it not to grow."

Here we have exhibited to us the nature of the everlasting covenant which God had made with David. We have here, in the first place, the expression that all his salvation, and all his desire, were concentrated in the fulfilment of this covenant; and, in the next place, we have the honest acknowledgment of the truth that his house was not in the condition that it shall be when God shall fulfill His covenant. Now, *what* and *where* was this throne of David which was to be established forever? and how far off was the time when it should be thus permanently established? Listen, now, to the great God upon this point. Turn to the 89th Psalm. Who is the speaker? The great God! Read from the 3d verse. I think the question will certainly be settled between me and my opponent on three or four points before we leave this psalm: "I have made a covenant with my chosen; I have sworn unto David my servant; thy seed will I establish forever, and build up my throne to all generations. Selah." Again, he says in the 27th, 28th and 29th verses: "Also, I will make him my first-born, higher than the kings of the earth. My mercy will I keep for him forevermore, and my covenant shall stand fast with him. His seed also will I make to endure forever, and his throne as the days of heaven."

The endless ages of eternity—for these are heaven's days—shall measure the duration of the throne and empire of the Son of God, and son of David, which he shall possess in fulfillment of the oath of the eternal and unchangeable Lord God. Again, he says in the 34th and following verses of this same psalm: "My covenant will I not break, nor alter the thing that is gone out of my lips. Once have I sworn by my holiness that I will not lie unto David. His seed shall endure forever and his throne as the sun before me. It shall be established forever as the moon, and as a faithful witness in heaven." As soon may we expect the moon to grow dim and fade from the heavens, and the sun to roll backward upon the fountains of light, as that God's oath and covenant shall be broken by separating Jesus Christ from the throne and kingdom of David.

I next introduce the prophet Isaiah as a witness upon these four points; first, *who* will be the king to reign over the kingdom forever; second, *where* will be his throne, and in *what* will it consist; third, *what* will be the character of his subjects, and *who* will they be, and fourth, how long will the kingdom continue.

You have heard already the testimony of the inspired prophet, the dying testimony of David, and the testimony of the Eternal God. I now call attention once more to the language of the prophet Isaiah. Wrapped in mystic vision he rolled back the curtains of time, and unfolded the future reign of David's royal Son. Five hundred years before his birth he says:

"For unto us a child is born, unto us a son is given; and the government shall be upon his shoulder; and his name shall be called Wonderful, Counseller, The mighty

God, The everlasting Father, The Prince of Peace. Of the increase of *his* government and peace *there shall be* no end, upon the throne of David, and upon his kingdom, to order it, and to establish it with judgment and with justice from henceforth even forever. The zeal of the Lord of hosts will perform this."

What assurance have we of the fulfillment of this glorious promise? "The zeal of the Lord of Hosts will perform this."

The next witness that I shall introduce to you is the Angel Gabriel. Descending from his high seat of glory he came to Mary just before this child is born—just before this Son is given, and says to her that she shall conceive and bring forth a son, and he shall be called the son of the Highest. That is just what Nathan told David. "He shall be called my son," said God, speaking through the mouth of Nathan his prophet. I take no issue with my opponent in regard to the endless duration of the Kingdom. He may emphasize the word 'forever' as much as he pleases—it is the *nature* of the kingdom of God, and not its endless duration, which forms the great gulf that separates us as far as Lazarus was separated from Dives.

Now there is not a church upon the face of the earth that does not accept the testimony of the Angel Gabriel on this point. There is not a person on the globe who would think of impeaching Gabriel's testimony, when he said a virgin should conceive and bring forth a son. It required nothing but naked faith in God's veracity. All the friends of Christianity—all the friends of the Bible believe it. All these statements they take literally. What is the matter that they must spiritualize all the glorious promises in regard to the Kingdom of God? The very same witness has given his testimony as in the other case, and under as solemn an obligation, and there is not a single broken link in the golden chain that binds Christ to David's throne, and gives him as the subjects of his rule, the twelve tribes of Israel, for ever and ever. Hear Gabriel's testimony in regard to the *nature* of the kingdom, as found in Luke 1st chap., 31st to 33d verses, inclusive:

"And, behold, thou shalt conceive in thy womb, and bring forth a son, and shalt call his name JESUS. He shall be great, and shall be called the Son of the Highest: and the Lord God shall give unto him the throne of his father David; And he shall reign over the house of Jacob forever; and of his kingdom there shall be no end."

Here Gabriel asserts the simple fact that the Lord God shall give unto Jesus Christ the throne of David. Why will our opponents insist upon impeaching their own witness? Will you receive the statement of the angel that a virgin should conceive and bring forth a son literally? Do you assert that this is figurative language? If not, what authority have you for the statement, that the throne of David, promised in the same connection, to Christ forever, is a *spiritual* throne, and not *literally* the throne of David? If one was *figurative* the other was also. We must either make *all* spiritual or *all* literal. If you would have a spiritual kingdom you must have a spiritual virgin, a mystical or spiritual son of God, and deny the whole thing as being a matter of fact transaction; or otherwise you must make it all literal. You must understand a literal virgin, a real son of God—he must be literally great and must reign literally on the throne of his father David. Make it all literal and all is plain, clear and satisfactory; nor can it be made so in any other way. If some such statement should be made in the present day to some virgin in America about the Presidential chair, or the city of Washington, or the government of the United States, would she think of spiritualizing it? We have no evidence that Mary had graduated in a modern theological school—she could have had no other view of David's throne and the house of Jacob, than that of David's kingly power in Jerusalem over the twelve tribes of Israel.

I will bring before you another witness, the Lord Jesus Christ. Go to the 19th chapter of Matthew, and 16th verse. A man had just come to Christ with sincerity and deep interest beaming from his noble countenance. We are told that when the Savior saw him he loved him. He said to the Savior; "Good master, what good thing shall I do that I may have eternal life?" Christ replied, "Why callest thou me good? there is none good but one, that is God; but if thou wilt enter into life keep the commandments." The response of the young man was, "all these have I kept from my youth up—what lack I yet?" Christ well knew where the idol was that the young man worshiped, and he said to him, "Go and sell that thou hast and give to the poor, and come and follow me." We are told that when the young man heard that he went away sorrowful, for he had great possessions. Peter said to Christ after he had departed, "Now Lord, we have left all and followed thee, what shall we have therefor?" Peter was anxious to know what kind of pay he was going to receive. Listen now to Christ's response to this inquiry. "Ye which have followed me, in the regeneration when the son of man shall sit in the throne of his glory, ye also shall sit upon twelve thrones, judging the twelve tribes of Israel." Here we have a confirmation of our glorious hope from the mouth of Christ himself. When the kingdom of God shall be set up, Christ shall be the King, and the twelve tribes of Israel his kingdom over which he shall rule.

In the next place, I appeal to the testimony of the wise men of the East, who followed the glittering star in heaven's dome until it stood still over the manger where the Son of God lay. They found him there. They bowed before him and worshiped him under the lofty title of King of the Jews.

The next witnesses I shall bring before you are Pontius Pilate and Christ. Paul declares, in reference to our Savior's testimony, that he bore a noble testimony before Pilate. Listen to the testimony he bore in reference to his title to the kingdom when he was standing as a condemned criminal before Pilate. Pilate said to him: "Art thou the King of the Jews?" Christ answered him in these words: "Thou sayest that I am king," which is equivalent to saying, "Thou sayest the truth." "To this end was I born, and for this cause came I into the world." John xviii: 37; 1st Tim. vi: 13. To what end was the Son of God born? And for what did he come into the world? For the purpose of being a king. Such was the testimony of the Son of God himself, uttered in the midst of the tragic scenes that preceded his death. I now want to add the testimony of the Roman Governor to that of Christ. It was the custom of the Romans, in every case of death by crucifixion, to write upon the cross the charge on which the criminal had been condemned to death. We will now have Pilate decide, as a judge, who the king and subjects of God's kingdom shall be. In three living, spoken languages, the three dominant languages of the world, at that time, Greek, Latin, and Hebrew, were written, in flaming characters, upon that cross, these words: "JESUS OF NAZARETH, THE KING OF THE JEWS." The infamy and the glory of the suffering Son of God unite in this declaration. "Nazareth" is expressive of his infamy —that he was "King of the Jews," expresses his glory. When I preach the cross of Christ I do not preach about the merit attached to two transfixed pieces of wood. There was no more saving power in the cross upon which the Savior died than there was in those of the two thieves who were crucified with him. The glory of the cross of Christ is comprehended in the testimony which Pilate bore in regard to the kingdom of God and the subjects of that kingdom when he wrote upon the cross this inscription: "Jesus of Nazareth, King of the Jews."

Where shall I go for testimony in regard to the kingdom of God if this will not decide the question? I will call your attention to only one more witness—to another kind of testimony—namely, that of Peter, on the day of Pentecost. Christ had died the death of the cross—he had entered the grave and lain there in Death's dominions for three days—he had risen from the tomb and for forty days had walked the earth and held communion with his disciples. He then prepared to take his leave of them. He urged upon them the great responsibility rest-ing upon them, of standing forth as God's representatives upon earth, through whom the Gospel should be made known to all the nations of the world. He commissioned them to go forth into all the world as the heralds of salvation, but directed them to tarry at Jerusalem until they should be endued with power from on high. And now the day of Pentecost had fully come, and power from heaven had fallen upon the disciples of the Lord. The Holy Ghost is poured out upon them, and in the midst of the wonderful and startling scenes that followed, Peter stood forth and preached the first Gospel sermon that ever was pronounced under the great commission—" Go ye into all the world and preach my Gospel to every creature "—and there were added unto the church, in one day, three thousand souls, out of seventeen different nations represented in the mighty gathering together of the people in the city of Jerusalem at the great feast of Pentecost. And permit me to say just here that I think I can easily discriminate between three thousand souls out of every nation under heaven and the nations themselves from which they came. The distinction is manifest and has no difficulty at all for me, nor will it have any for my friend if he is willing to understand it aright. Peter commences his sermon. He tells the Jews that they had with wicked hands crucified the Prince of Life and hanged him on a tree. " Whom God hath raised up, having loosed the pains of death, because it was not possible that he should be holden of it." Why was it not possible for death to fasten its iron fangs upon the Savior forever? Had Death not held dominion over the whole human race for four thousand years? Turn to the 2d chapter of Acts where this transaction is recorded, and there, in the 30th verse, you will find the reason why death could not hold dominion over the son of the Living God forever. God's oath and covenant were involved; and sooner would heaven and earth pass than these should fail. See Acts ii: 30: "Therefore, being a prophet, and knowing that God had sworn, with an oath to him, that of the fruit of his loins, according to the flesh, he would raise up Christ to sit on his throne." And Psalms 132: 11: "The Lord hath sworn in truth unto David; he will not turn from it; of the fruit of thy body will I set upon thy throne." And in the 37th verse of this same chapter, we learn the result of this language on the part of Peter. When he had clearly proved to them that in putting to death Jesus Christ they had not simply rid the world of a "pestilent fellow," but that they had killed God's annointed one—him who was ordained of God to occupy David's throne—crucified their own national hope and the destined monarch of the world. Then it was that conviction seized upon their hearts and they cried out: "Men and brethren, what shall we do?"

What was the great turning point, the climax of this great gospel sermon? The culminating point of the apostle's theme was the fulfillment of God's promises in raising up Christ from the dead, in order that in due time he should sit upon David's throne and rule over the twelve tribes of Israel; for the same oath and covenant which pledges the great Jehovah to place his Son upon David's throne, and retain him there while the sun and moon shall shine, and while the days of heaven shall roll on, equally pledges him to give him David's kingdom forever. The import of that great revival sermon on that august occasion, was the fulfillment of the oath and covenant of God, in placing Christ upon David's throne and kingdom. But when this oath and covenant shall be verified, the Son of God and the royal son of David will be the *king*, and the twelve tribes of Israel will be the subjects of the kingdom of God. Christ is the legal heir to David's throne. Though all the prophecies should center in him, still, unless his legitimacy as David's legal successor could be sustained, his title cannot be validated.

In Matthew, 1st chapter, we find a long line of royal ancestors, in which the legal genealogy of Christ may be be traced back to David's throne. In Luke, 3d chapter, we find another line of genealogy leading back to David. One line runs from Joseph, the legal father of Christ, and the other line from Heli, the father of Mary, its not being customary to recon the genealogy of women. One of these lines of genealogy descended from David through Solomon his royal son, and the other through Nathan the prophet. These lines run parallel until united in the house of Zorobabel; then branching out, they run like two parallel lines until they are united in Joseph and Mary; since which the Jews have never chronicled David's genealogy. These lines were legally united by the marriage of Joseph and Mary, and Christ being their firstborn, has all the right, legally and naturally, to David's throne. And having ascended to heaven with issue, he has the keys to David's throne; he can open and no man can shut, and when he shuts no man can open. He is heir to David's literal throne and kingdom.

### AFF.—P. T. RUSSELL—FOURTH SPEECH.

We first call attention to the simple truth that David never owned a throne in his own right; that is to say, the right of property never was in him, but in another, and it was his only by right of occupancy—as this stand is now mine by the same right. Turn to 1st Chornicles, 29th chapter and 23d verse. It reads as follows:

"Then Solomon sat on the throne of the Lord as king instead of David his father, and prospered; and all Israel obeyed him."

Here the declaration is made that the throne upon which David sat was the Lord's throne. We wish this fact kept fully in mind from this time on. Perhaps we shall not mention it again until our final closing speech.

I now invite your attention to the 32d chapter of Isaiah, where you will find abundant and overwhelming proof that the kingdom of the Messiah should exist contemporaneously with a state of probation:

"Behold, a king shall reign in righteousness, and princes shall rule in judgment. And a man shall be as a hiding place from the wind, and a covert from the tempest; as rivers of water in a dry place, as the shadow of a great rock in a weary land. And the eyes of them that see shall not be dim, and the ears of them that hear shall hearken. The heart also of the rash shall understand knowledge, and the tongue of the stammerers shall be ready to speak plainly. The vile person shall be no more called liberal, nor the churl said to be bountiful. For the vile person will speak villany, and his heart will work iniquity, to practice hypocrisy, and to utter error against the Lord, to make empty the soul of the hungry; and he will cause the drink of the thirsty to fail. The instruments also of the churl are evil: he deviseth wicked devices to destroy the poor with lying words, even when the needy speaketh right."

Such shall be the condition of things among the nations of the earth at the very time when this king shall reign and prosper. "The vile person will still speak villainy, and his heart will work iniquity," and during this very time the king here spoken of shall reign and prosper. His reign therefore is now, in a state of probation, and not hereafter, when a state of probation shall no longer exist.

I wish in the next place to call your attention to Isaiah, 9th chapter, 6th and 7th verses, with reference especially to the hight and degree of this prosperity:

"For unto us a child is born, unto us a son is given: and the government shall be upon his shoulder: and his his name shall be called Wonderful, Counsellor, The Mighty God, The everlasting Father, The Prince of Peace. Of the increase of his government and peace there shall be no end, upon the throne of David, and upon his kingdom, to order it, and to establish it with judgment and with justice from henceforth even for ever. The zeal of the Lord of hosts will perform this."

Here the one single thought that I wish to fasten upon your minds is this; "Of the increase of his government and peace there shall be no end." We have already found the beginning of his government. Here it is spoken of as *increasing*. I can imagine only three ways in which a government can increase: first, by the increase of its territory; second by the increase of power in the hands of the ruler; and third, by the increase in the number of its citizens. By one or all of these ways a kingdom may increase, and in no other way. How, therefore, may the kingdom of God increase? It cannot increase by the increase of power in the hands of the ruler, because Matthew, in the 28th chapter of his gospel, and at the 18th verse, tells us that "Jesus came and spake unto them saying, All power is given unto me in heaven and in earth." Hence there can be no increase of this kingdom through an increase of power in the hands of the ruler. We turn once more and ask, could the kingdom increase through an increase in the extent of its territorial area? I answer, no. The sceptre of the king already sways rightfully over all heaven and earth; hence, no such thing is possible as an increase of his territory.

There is but one single process remaining, and that is by an increase in the number of the subjects of the kingdom. And I know of only two ways in which the number of subjects of a government can be increased: one of them is the way in which kingdoms of an earthly nature increase the number of their subjects, and we cannot expect the kingdom of Christ, which is not of this world, to increase in that manner. There is but one way left for the increase of subjects of this kingdom, and that is by what is called in common parlance, being "born again," or if you please, *conversion*. This is to be the process of its growth and increase, for the kingdom is to be a spiritual and not a fleshly one.

Turn, now, and look at Daniel, 2d chapter and 35th verse, where we have an idea of the origin and beginning of this kingdom, under the similitude of a small stone cut from the mountain side without hands, which smote the great image upon its feet, and then beginning to expand, became a great mountain and filled the whole earth. We have already said enough to indicate what the nature of the process is, by which this growth is to be effected. Turn, now, if you please, to Acts, 1st chapter and 15th verse, and there you will learn that on the day of Pentecost the number of the subjects of Christ's kingdom was about an hundred and twenty; and as they were assembled with one accord in one place, (as we are told in the succeeding chapter) suddenly there came a sound from heaven as of a rushing mighty wind, and it filled all the house where they were sitting. It was the trump of redeeming grace and dying love. The Holy Spirit was poured out in rich effusion, in order that the people might be prepared to bow in submission to that divine law which was soon to go forth from Zion, and thus be translated into the kingdom of God's dear Son. The royal banner of the Prince of Peace was here unfurled, and three thousand souls were added to the Church— were born into that kingdom that same day. The kingdom was beginning to grow. In its commencement it had only an hundred and twenty citizens, or subjects, upon the face of the earth, but on the very first day that the battle was gained, three thousand surrendered at discretion and bowed themselves in submission and allegiance to him who "hath upon his vesture and upon his thigh a name written, "KING OF KINGS AND LORD OF LORDS. Add, now, the three thousand converts to the original number of the subjects of Christ's Kingdom, and you find that so rapidly has the Kingdom of God grown and increased, that ere the sun goes down it numbers three thousand one hundred and twenty souls.

Turn, now, to Acts, 4th chapter and 4th verse, and here again we find the royal banner of King Immanuel unfurled, and many of them that heard the word believed, "and the number of the men was about five thousand. Add this number to the number of those who had submitted to the authority of the King when the sun set on the day of Pentecost, and we find the Kingdom has increased until it embraces the goodly number of eight thousand one hundred and twenty souls. Pass on a little further in this interesting history, and in the 5th chapter we find that believers were still added to the Lord—"multitudes both of men and women." In the 28th verse of this 5th chapter we find the High Priest telling the apostles that they had "filled all Jerusalem with this doctrine." And so the gospel spread, the Kingdom of God increased. Samaria and Gallilee heard the glad tidings of salvation and bowed in submission to God's Son, and were translated into his kingdom, and the uttermost parts of the earth are made vocal with the high-sounding praises of Immanuel. The Kingdom of Heaven, said the Savior, is like unto a little leaven which a woman took and hid in three measures of meal until the whole was leavened. Daniel also brings forcibly and irresistibly before our minds the same characteristic mark of this kingdom, under the figure of a small stone which enlarged, and grew, and expanded until it became a great mountain and filled the whole earth. As long as the glorious gospel of the Prince of Peace shall be preached upon this earth, men will submit to its authority, and thus onward and onward still in triumph this sublime institution will move, until earth's hills and valleys shall become vocal with the praises of the King Immanuel.

The time will come, however, when the solemn declaration will go forth from the presence of him who is alpha and omega, the beginning and the end, the first and the last, " Let him who is unjust be unjust still, and he that is filthy let him be filthy still, and he that is righteous let him be righteous still, and he that is holy let him be holy still. Then shall come the end of all things according to the language of 1st Corinthians, 15th chapter, and 24th and 25th verses:

"Then cometh the end, when he shall have delivered up the kingdom to God, even the Father when he shall have put down all rule, and all authority and power; for he must reign, till he hath put all enemies under his feet."

Here we have tracked the course of the reign of Christ from his coronation till the time when, in the graphic language of Paul, "the last enemy is subdued under his feet." This measures all the space of time complete and entire from the time of Christ's ascension into heaven, mentioned in Acts, 1st chapter, down to the time when all things shall be subdued unto him, mentioned in 1st Cor. 15th chapter. "Then cometh the end, when he shall have delivered up the Kingdom to God, even the Father, when he shall have put down all rule, and authority and power." Here we have next in order the giving up of the kingdom. Now what kingdom is it that is thus to be given up to the Father? If I should give this little manuscript which I now hold in my hand to one of my audience would it not be the same thing it is now? Undoubtedly it would. The transfer would not change it a particle. And when the time appointed shall come, and the Son shall render up to the Father the kingdom he had been in possession of, will it not be the same and none other? Certainly it will. The Son is to give up the kingdom to the Father, and in order that he may give up the kingdom to the Father he must have been in the possession of that kingdom.

I now call your attention to Acts 3d chapter, 20th and 21st verses: "And he shall send Jesus Christ, which before was preached unto you; whom the heaven must receive until the times of restitution of all things, which God hath spoken by the mouth of all his holy prophets since the world began."

Here mark particularly this one simple fact, that when the Savior went to heaven he was to sit there on the right hand of the Father, until all that had been spoken by the prophets since the world began should be accomplished. Do you recollect the prophecy of the introduction of a new heaven and a new earth—John saw it in prophetic vision, as it is recorded in the 1st verse of the 21st chapter of Revelations: "And I saw a new heaven and a new earth; for the first heaven and the first earth were passed away, and there was no more sea." If therefore, the Son is to remain at the right hand of the Father on high until all that was spoken by the prophets should be fulfilled, there he is to remain then until the moving away of the present heaven and of the present earth, and the introduction of the new. Turn now to the 2d Epistle of Paul to Timothy, and read the first verse of the 4th chapter. "I charge thee therefore before God, and the Lord Jesus Christ, who shall judge the quick and the dead at his appearing and his kingdom."

Here you see that Christ is to judge both the living and the dead at the time of his appearing and kingdom. The term, "the dead" embraces all the dead. Every human being is to be brought out from under death's dominion and death's power to be demolished. Then is he to judge both the living and the dead, sitting upon the throne of his kingdom. Turn again to Matthew, 25th chapter, 31st verse, and thence on.

"When the son of man shall come in his glory, and all the holy angels with him, then shall he sit upon the throne of his glory; and before him shall be gathered all nations; and he shall separate them one from another, as a shepherd divideth his sheep from the goats; And he shall set the sheep on his right hand, but the goats on the left."

Notice here that the time here spoken of as the time of his appearing and kingdom, is identically the same with the time of his coming to judge the living and the dead, *i. e.*, the whole world.

Go with me now to 2d Thessalonians 2d chapter, 1st and 2d verses: "Now we beseech you, brethren, by the coming of our Lord Jesus Christ, and by our gathering together unto him, That ye be not soon shaken in mind, or be troubled, neither by spirit, nor by word, nor by letter as from us, as that the day of Christ is at hand."

The Thessalonians, to whom this letter of the Apostle is addressed, had become somewhat discomposed by the idea that the second coming of the Savior was quite near at hand. Paul learned this and he here attempts to instruct them better. Pass on to the 8th verse of this same chapter: "And then shall that wicked be revealed, whom the Lord shall consume with the spirit of his mouth, and shall destroy with the brightness of his coming."

The "man of sin" is to be destroyed at this time—the time of the Lord's second coming, when the dead are to be raised, for "all that are in their graves shall hear his voice and shall come forth," and he is then to judge both the living and the dead. He is then to separate the righteous from the wicked as a shepherd divideth his sheep from the goats. The condition of every human being is to be then finally and forever fixed. And this is the emphatic reason why St. Peter says to his brethren: "For so shall an entrance be administered unto us abundantly into the *everlasting* kingdom of our Lord and Savior Jesus Christ." From this point onward the Gospel banner is to be no more unfurled—no more offers of mercy are to be extended—the proclamation goes forth, "He that is filthy let him be filthy still," and the wicked are driven away in their wickedness, banished forever from the presence of the Lord and the glory of his power. The Son of God sitting upon the throne of his glory as the judge of all the earth, says to those on his right hand, in this the day of his coming, "come ye blessed of my Father inherit the kingdom prepared for you from the foundation of the world." All these things we have concentrating right at the time of "his coming." It is at this particular time, the time of "his coming," that the elements are to melt with fervent heat, the heavens are to be rolled together like a scroll, the present heavens and earth are to move aside with a great noise and give room for a new heaven and a new earth. All these sublime events concentrating as they do upon the very time called in the passages I have just read to you, "the time of his coming," all testify to the truth, that when the son of man shall come a second time there can be no such thing as an earthly kingdom upon this globe.

I will here examine what is supposed to be a difficulty. I may be asked this question: Is not the Lord to come at the time of the first resurrection? I answer, No. It is at the time of the second resurrection that his coming shall take place. None but those who suffered death by violence for their advocacy of the truth will be found in the first resurrection. Read Revelations, 20th chapter, 4th and 7th verses, inclusive. "And I saw thrones, and they sat upon them, and judgment was given unto them: and I saw the souls of them that were beheaded for the witness of Jesus, and for the word of God, and which had not worshipped the beast, neither his image, neither had received his mark upon their foreheads, or in their hands; and they lived and reigned with Christ a thousand years. But the rest of the dead lived not again until the thousand years were finished. This is the first resurrection. Blessed and holy is he that hath part in the first resurrection: on such the second death hath no power, but they shall be priests of God and of Christ, and shall reign with him a thousand years. And when the thousand years are expired, Satan shall be loosed out of his prison."

Here we have presented the very idea that I desire to bring before you — that none but the old martyrs shall be found in the first resurrection. Examine if you please the description that is given us of the last and final resurrection, found in the same chapter and at the 12th verse: "And I saw the dead, small and great stand before God; and the books were opened; and another book was open, which is the book of life; and the dead were judged out of those things which were written in the books, according to their works.

Then in the verses following, the Revelator tells us where the dead come from.

"And the sea gave up the dead which were in it; and death and hell delivered up the dead which were in them; and they were judged every man according to their works." Mark the 15th verse: "And whosoever was not found written in the book of life was cast into the lake of fire."

Why are these words used in reference to the end of a certain class of persons? Are there not some who will be found in the last resurrection whose names are recorded in the Lamb's book of life? It is clear that there are. There will be both righteous and wicked concerned in the second resurrection, while none but the old martyrs will be found to have a part in the first, God calling them up from the grave before the general resurrection, in order to reward them for the sufferings they had endured, while the rest of the race shall still be wrapped in the slumbers of the tomb, and "they shall live and reign with Christ a thousand years." We should not fail to observe, however, that while the assertion is made that these having part in the first resurrection shall live and reign with Christ a thousand years, the word *with* does not always indicate or signify personal presence. Paul says of himself and his brethren, "we were buried with him in baptism." Does the word *with*, as there employed signify actual personal presence? No—nor does it signify actual personal presence in the passage before us—for we are told in a passage of scripture to which your attention has been frequently called during the progress of this discussion, that the son shall remain at the right hand of the Father, until death, the last enemy is despoiled of all his power—until the last human being has burst death's bars and passed from under his dominion. Therefore we conclude that the word "with" when used with reference to Christ and those who are to have a place in the first resurrection, does not imply his actual personal presence with them, but it is to be understood in another and a different sense.

## NEG.—J. M. STEPHENSON—FOURTH SPEECH.

There was only one objection advanced by my opponent to any position I have taken. I have attempted to prove only two points, viz: that the King will be Jesus of Nazareth, and that the subjects will be the twelve tribes of Israel. All the testimony that has thus far been brought forward upon either side of this controversy demonstrates this truth. I wish now to call your attention to another point, to demonstrate that it is the *literal* kingdom of

Israel, and not a spiritual kingdom represented under that name—that it is a literal kingdom and not a spiritual church. Turn, if you please, to the prophecy of Ezekiel, 21st chapter, 25th, 26th and 27th verses:

"And thou, profane wicked prince of Israel, whose day is come, when iniquity *shall have* an end. Thus saith the Lord God; Remove the diadem, and take off the crown: this *shall* not *be* the same: exalt *him that is* low, and abase *him that is* high.

"I will overturn, overturn, overturn it; and it shall be. no *more*, until he come whose right it is; and I will give it *him*."

"I will overturn it,"—the kingdom—" and it shall be no, more until he come whose right it is, and I will give it to, him." Here we find predicted the restoration of the very same kingdom, which had passed through these subversions alluded to in the language immediately preceding it. "I will overturn, overturn, overturn *it*, and *it* shall be no more. It is to be no more *until* a certain event shall take place. Now, if it be true that this kingdom is to be subverted *forever*, *why* does the prophet of God here use the adverb "*until?*" That adverb "until" demonstrates to us that the same kingdom which was to be beyond a doubt overturned is to be *restored*, and that then its subversion shall cease. The plain assertion of the Lord is not merely, I will overturn *it*, but also, I will give *it* to him whose right it is; and until he come the kingdom shall be subverted and no longer. Hence we see that the same kingdom over which Zedekiah reigned—the same kingdom overturned by the Roman armies—the same kingdom that is now under the hand of Gentile power shall be given to him who, has a right to the possession of that kingdom—the Lord Jesus Christ.

How can that be if the kingdom here spoken of means, that church? Was the church overturned? Was the church given to Christ on the day of Pentecost? To, *restore* anything is to re-establish, and bring back again, the same thing that had been destroyed or subverted. The church of God was not overturned but the kingdom.

that was overturned was the literal kingdom of Israel, and that is the kingdom that is to be *restored* and given to Jesus Christ. Did Zedekiah reign over the church which was set up on the day of Pentecost? It was the literal kingdom of Israel which passed through these series of subversions; it must therefore be the literal kingdom that will be given to Christ. He, and he alone has a right to the literal kingdom of David. I have demonstrated by the mouth of the eternal God himself. I have proven by the testimony of Jesus Christ, and of Peter, and of Gabriel that Jesus of Nazareth is the rightful heir to Zedekiah's kingdom. I have demonstrated it by two lines of genealogy, running in parallel lines from David down through all the intervening generations, until we find them meeting in the Messiah, and have thus proven that he alone is of right entitled to sit upon "the throne of his father David." Does not this fully demonstrate the literal character of this kingdom?

We are told by the inspired prophets, that when the twelve tribes of Israel shall be re-united into one nation, they shall never more be plucked up out of the land. They shall possess the land forever, and Christ shall reign over them. Now the kingdom of Christ is to continue for ever and ever. My opponent would have us believe that that kingdom must run co-extensive with a state of endless probation, and that *his* church kingdom shall increase by the process of conversion. As the kingdom, when once established is to continue forever and ever, as a natural consequence, and as a legitimate and unavoidable sequence from my opponent's own position, there will be a state of probation forever and a succession of conversions forever and ever. Does he admit that? If he does not, then his objection rests with equal force against his own position. This objection, whether applied to the church or the kingdom would prove endless probation. I will ask my opponent if it is true that the increase of the church went on continuously after the day of Pentecost? Certainly not. Under Nero the church of God was reduced to a mere handful of men and women. Hence we see that the church set up on the day of Pentecost was not the kingdom which was promised to Jesus Christ by all the holy prophets. The Apostles asked Christ a question expressive of their firm faith in the literal character of his kingdom: "Wilt thou at this time restore the kingdom to Israel?" Was it the church that they meant? Was the church then subverted? No sincere inquirer after truth can fail to be convinced at a single glance that they referred to a literal kingdom—the kingdom that was at that time in a state of subversion—the kingdom of Israel restored. But what does Christ say to them in reply to this inquiry? He said to them: "It is not for you to know the times nor the seasons which the Father hath put in his own power. What *times* and *seasons* was it not their privilege to know? The times and seasons when the great event should occur in regard to which they had just inquired—the *time* when the kingdom should be restored to Israel, thus clearly intimating that that time should come. If the kingdom is to be "restored" according to the plain teachings of the word of God, it will be that kingdom which before existed, for no kingdom can be restored except that which before existed, and which was for the time being subverted or "overturned."

But my opponent says David never had a throne. Isaiah disagrees with him, for he says, in relation to the Messiah, that "of the increase of his government and peace there shall be no end *upon the throne of David.*" And the angel Gabriel, when he appeared to the Virgin Mary, said to her, "and the Lord God shall give unto him the *throne* of his father David:" Where is the propriety of this language, if "David's throne" had never existed—if David, as my opponent declares, never had a throne? It is impossible to reconcile or harmonize the teachings of the word of God upon any other hypothesis than that Jesus Christ is to be a literal king upon a literal throne—the throne of David. The original words rendered throne in Hebrew and Greek denote regal power and glory.

I now call your attention to the third element of the kingdom of God—the territory of the kingdom. I shall refer to only a few texts in support of my position upon this point. All the texts advanced by my opponent I am ready to adopt as my own, and to stand or fall by them, for I know that the truth of God cannot contradict itself when we interpret it aright. In the territory promised by the Almighty to Abraham "for an everlasting covenant," we have the first view of the territory of the kingdom of Jesus Christ. In the 2d Chapter of Daniel, where the kingdom is represented under the figure of a stone, which became a great mountain and filled the whole earth, we have the same thing again presented to our minds. If the kingdom is not to grow how can it be appropriately represented by a stone growing until it fills the whole world? In accordance with this is the language of the 7th Chapter of Daniel, where it is said that "there was given to him dominion, and glory, and a kingdom, that all people, nations and languages should serve him." Where is that kingdom to be located? All nations, and people, and tongues are to be subject unto it. The whole earth is to be its domain. "And the kingdom and dominion, and the greatness of the kingdom under the whole heaven shall be given to the Saints of the Most High, whose kingdom is an everlasting kingdom, and all dominions shall serve and obey him." The prayer which Christ taught his disciples affords another proof of the locality of the kingdom of Jesus Christ. He taught them to say, "Thy kingdom come." The kingdom is to come to us, we are not to go to it.

There are two ways, and only two, of possessing a kingdom. One is by legitimate heirship, the other by conquest. Jesus Christ, being the son of David, shall inherit David's throne. And having, as I think, clearly demonstrated the truth that Jesus Christ shall sit upon David's throne, which is his by legitimate inheritance, let me ask this great and vitally important question: "Will the Lord Jesus Christ govern this kingdom alone?" He will present an anomaly to all other rulers, if he does. His kingdom will be an exception to all the other kingdoms that have ever existed on the face of the earth, if he does. It will be without example and without precedent. No, my friends, the Lord Jesus Christ, when he shall sit on the throne of his kingdom, will not rule that kingdom alone. He will have a royal cabinet that shall share with him the duties of government and the administration of the laws. I am sorry that every member of the Disciple Church is not here to-day to hear the glorious truth that God has revealed in his word to them that will understand it aright —that Christ's believing followers are to reign with him. Hence our Savior says to his disciples: "It is your Father's good pleasure to give to you the *kingdom*." Now for the proof in the case.

Let me call your attention first to the language of Christ when the mother of Zebedee's children came to him and asked, as a special favor, that her two sons might sit, one on his right hand and the other on his left, when he should sit upon the throne of his kingdom. Jesus said: "Are ye able to drink of the cup that I shall drink of, and to be baptized with the baptism that I am baptized with?" They said unto him: "We are able." Then said Jesus unto them: "Ye shall indeed drink of my cup," &c., "but to sit on my right hand and on my left is not mine to give, but it shall be given to them for whom it is prepared of my Father." Thus Christ himself admitted that the Father had reserved positions and places of honor in his kingdom for those whom he deemed worthy of such distinction. This is from Matthew, 20th chapter, 20th, 21st, 22d, and 23d verses. And again we read that upon another occasion Christ, in answer to a question asked by Peter, said: "Ye that have followed me, in the regeneration when the son of man shall sit in the throne of his glory, ye also shall sit upon twelve thrones judging the twelve tribes of Israel." Matthew, 19th chapter and 28th verse. Just so sure as Christ shall sit upon his throne—the throne of David, and rule over the twelve tribes of Israel—just so sure shall his twelve apostles also sit upon twelve thrones and share with him the glory of his kingdom.

Turn now to the 2d chapter of Paul's second letter to Timothy, and at the 12th verse we shall find Timothy brought in as a connecting link between the disciples of our Lord and us. Timothy, also, is to reign with Christ. Says Paul: "If we suffer, we shall also reign with him." Mark the language. Paul does not tell Timothy that if we suffer we shall be subjects of his kingdom merely, or that we shall have the privilege of being reigned over by Christ, but he says "we shall reign with him." How shall we understand this passage of the Word of God? It must be taken either figuratively or literally. If one part is taken literally all must be so taken. If one part is interpreted figuratively all must be interpreted in like manner. Which will you do? Will you make the suffering here spoken of literal? If you do, then you must yield the point that the reign with Christ is also literal. You can not, by any rule of interpretation, make one literal and the other figurative. The saints shall reign, therefore, just as truly and as literally as Christ himself shall reign. The word reign, in Greek, signifies royalty. Do subjects share the royalty of their king? Do subjects reign? Do the subjects of Queen Victoria *reign with her?* To assert such a thing would be to ignore the true import of all language.

Turn, now, to the 2d chapter of Revelations, 26th and 27th verses. There Christ says to the church: "And he that overcometh, and keepeth my works unto the end, to him will I give power over the nations; and he shall rule them with a rod of iron; as a vessels of the potter shall they be broken to shivers; even as I received of my Father."

Let us go back now to the origin of Christ's original title to the throne, and ask on what conditions Christ is authorized to break in pieces the rebellious nations of the world. You will find it in the 2d Psalm, 7th, 8th and 9th verses: "I will declare the decree: The Lord hath said unto me, Thou art my son; this day have I begotten thee. Ask of me, and I shall give thee the heathen for thine inheritance, and the uttermost parts of the earth for thy possession. Thou shalt break them with a rod of iron; thou shalt dash them in pieces like a potter's vessel."

But on what conditions? Listen again. You will find in close connection the following language:

"Be wise now therefore, O ye kings; be instructed, ye judges of the earth. Serve the Lord with fear, and rejoice with trembling. Kiss the Son lest he be angry, and and ye perish from the way, when his wrath is kindled but a little. Blessed are all they that put their trust in him."

If the great kings and potentates of the world shall heed the voice of God what shall follow? "Blessed are all they that put their trust in him." Hence we see that Christ has the right to rule the nations of the earth, and that he will share that right with his believing followers, we are assured from the language already quoted from Revelations, 2d chapter, 26th and 27th verses:

"And he that overcometh, and keepeth my works unto the end, to him will I give power over nations; And he shall rule them with a rod of iron; as the vessels of a potter shall they be broken to shivers; even as I received of my Father."

Let us now go to the 5th chapter of Revelations and see what evidence there is contained in it upon the subject of the saints of God reigning with Christ when he shall possess the kingdom. I now bring before you a great multitude of witnesses, and witnesses too who will be believed. My opponent himself will agree with me that the redeemed host of God's elect cannot be mistaken in regard to the things whereof they speak.

"And one of the elders saith unto me, Weep not: behold, the Lion of the tribe of Juda, the Root of David, hath prevailed to open the book, and to loose the seven seals thereof. And I beheld, and, lo, in the midst of the elders, stood a Lamb as it had been slain, having seven horns and seven eyes, which are the seven spirits of God sent forth into all the earth. And he came and took the book out of the right hand of him that sat upon the throne. And when he had taken the book, the four beasts and four and twenty elders fell down before the Lamb, having every one of them harps, and golden vials full of odors, which are the prayers of saints. And they sung a new song, saying, Thou art worthy to take the book, and to open the seals thereof; for thou wast slain, and hast redeemed us to God by thy blood out of every kindred, and tongue, and people, and nation; And hast made us unto our God kings and priests; and we shall reign on the earth."

Do these saints of God speak the truth? If they do, then they are to reign, and if they are to reign then the earth will be the locality of their kingdom and reign; for "we shall reign in the earth." No stronger, plainer, or more pointed language can be found in the book of God than this, to prove that Christ will reign.

Turn now to the 20th chapter of Revelations and read the language of the 4th verse. Thrones are here seen looming up in the future.

"And I saw thrones, and they sat upon them, and judgment was given unto them; and I saw the souls of them that were beheaded for the witness of Jesus, and for the word of God, and which had not worshiped the beast, neither his image, neither had received his mark upon their foreheads, or in their hands; and they lived and reigned with Christ a thousand years."

A pronoun is used in order to avoid the repetition of a noun. The antecedent always goes before its pronoun. In this verse the saints of the most High God are the antecedent to which the first pronoun 'they' refers: "*they* sat upon thrones." Who sat upon these thrones? Not the "souls of them that were beheaded for the witness of Jesus," for they had not yet been mentioned and could not therefore be the antecedent of the pronoun THEY.

"But the rest of the dead lived not again until the thousand years were finished. This is the first resurrection. Blessed and holy is he that hath part in the first resurrection, on such the second death hath no power, but they shall be priests of God and of Christ, and shall reign with him a thousand years."

We see at a glance that the saints of the most High God will not only enjoy the privilege of reigning with

Christ as joint emperors of the world, but that they will occupy the same position that he does, and thus Christ while he will share the dominion as other rulers have done—will at the same time have a different cabinet from any other kingdom that ever existed; a royal cabinet—a kingly cabinet. The poorest Christian that walks the earth is a prince in disguise. This glory—this royalty is to be given to all the saints of the most High God.

Turn now to the 7th chapter of Daniel. One of the best Hebrew scholars in the United States declares that the words "Ancient of Days," used in the 9th and 13th verses of this chapter, may quite as appropriately and properly be applied to the angels of God who shouted aloud for joy when the foundations of the earth were laid, as to God the Father. The meaning, therefore, plainly is that the Lord Jesus Christ comes at the time here spoken of to these ancient ones, and there is given unto him dominion and glory and a kingdom, etc. Evidently, the kingdom and dominion referred to here is the kingdom of Israel which shall be restored to Christ and the dominion which he shall exercise over the nations of earth.

Turn to the 27th verse of the same chapter, and you will find the same promise made to all the saints of the Most High, which had, at the 13th and 14th verses, been made to Christ.

"And the kingdom and dominion, and the greatness of the kingdom under the whole heaven, shall be given to the people of the saints of the Most High, whose kingdom is an everlasting kingdom, and all dominions shall serve and obey him."

## AFF.—P. T. RUSSELL—FIFTH SPEECH.

### Second Day, Monday, October 1, 1866.

I shall call attention first to the position assumed by my opponent on Saturday, with reference to the Adamic charter of dominion. This requires, however, no argument upon my part inasmuch as the point was surrendered by my opponent by the admission which he made that Adam had forfeited all right to dominion by his transgression. It need not be followed any further.

In the next place I call your attention to the two distinct promises made to Abraham, to whom was given the distinguishing honor of standing before the world in all coming time as the head and representative of the faithful. The one promise was the promise of the Messiah and of the proffer of salvation through him to a dying world—the other was the promise to Abraham and his descendants, of the possession of the land of Palestine with all its privileges and appurtenances.

These are two distinct and separate matters. The first, embodying the promise of the Messiah, found in Genesis, 12th chapter, 1st and 3d verses inclusive, is in this form:

"Now the Lord said unto Abram, Get thee out of thy country, and from thy kindred, and thy father's house, unto a land that I will shew thee: and I will make of thee a great nation, and I will bless thee, and make thy name great; and thou shalt be a blessing: and I will bless them that bless thee, and curse him that curseth thee: and in thee shall all families of the earth be blessed."

Mark the important idea that is here embodied in the simple expression. "In thee shall all the families of the earth be blessed."

The next passage that we invite your attention to is Genesis, 15th chapter and 17th verse:

"And it came to pass, that, when the sun went down, and it was dark, behold a smoking furnace, and a burning lamp that passed between those pieces."

Connect this with Genesis, 17th chapter, from the 1st to the 14th verses inclusive:

"And when Abram was ninety years old and nine, the Lord appeared to Abram, and said unto him, I am the Almighty God; walk before me and be thou perfect. And I will make my covenant between me and thee, and will multiply thee accordingly. And Abram fell on his face, and God talked with him, saying, As for me, behold my covenant is with thee, and thou shalt be a father of many nations. Neither shall thy name any more be called Abram, but thy name shall be Abraham; for a father of many nations have I made thee. And I will make thee exceeding fruitful, and I will make nations of thee, and kings shall come out of thee. And I will establish my covenant between me and thee, and thy seed after thee in their generations for an everlasting covenant, to be a God unto thee, and to thy seed after thee. And I will give unto thee, and to thy seed after thee, the land wherein thou art a stranger, all the land of Canaan, for an everlasting possession; and I will be their God.

"And God said unto Abraham, Thou shalt keep my covenant therefore, thou and thy seed after thee in their generations. This is my covenant, which ye shall keep, between me and you and thy seed after thee; every man child among you shall be circumcised. And ye shall circumcise the flesh of your foreskin; and it shall be a token of the covenant betwixt me and you. And he that is eight days old shall be circumcised among you, every man child in your generations, he that is born in the house, or bought with money of any stranger, which is not of thy seed. He that is born in thy house, and he that is bought with thy money, must needs be circumcised: and my covenant shall be in your flesh, an everlasting covenant. And the uncircumcised man child whose flesh of his foreskin is not circumcised, that soul shall be cut off from his people; he hath broken my covenant."

Observe that in one passage, Genesis, 12th chapter, 2d verse, the word "nation" is used, being the singular number; while in the other passage, Genesis, 17th chapter, the word is used in the plural—"I will make nations of thee, and kings shall come out of thee."

There are two thoughts that I wish to fasten just here; first, not a solitary male has any right to anything that is promised in this covenant recorded in the 17th chapter of Genesis, unless he is circumcised; secondly, those who were thus circumcised, and no others, had the promise in this covenant of an earthly inheritance—the land of Palestine. And of this covenant of circumcision it was said in the 13th verse, "and my covenant shall be in your flesh for an everlasting covenant."

Having said enough to bring out before your minds the idea of the two distinctive features of this covenant, I will reread the 14th verse:

"And the uncircumcised man child whose flesh of his foreskin is not circumcised, that soul shall be cut of from his people; he hath broken my covenant."

By the breach of this covenant of circumcision there was a perpetual forfeiture of all its benefits. This language renders secure and permanent the truth that none but the circumcised have a right to an earthly inheritance by virtue of the promise made to Abraham at the time this covenant was made; while on the other hand, the other promise recorded in Genesis, 12th chapter, being wholly spiritual in its character, was common to all coming generations, as shown by the language, "in thee and in thy seed shall all the nations of the earth be blessed."

Connect this with the language found in Genesis, 26th chapter, commencing with the 1st verse and ending with the 4th verse:

"And there was a famine in the land, beside the first famine that was in the days of Abraham. And Isaac went unto Abimelech king of the Philistines unto Gerar. And the Lord appeared unto him, and said, Go down into Egypt; dwell in the land which I shall tell the of. Sojourn in this land, and I will be with thee; for unto thee, and unto thy seed, I will give all these countries, and I will perform the oath which I sware unto Abraham thy father; and I will make thy seed to multiply as the stars of heaven, and will give unto thy seed all these countries; and in thy seed shall all the nations of the earth be blessed."

Here we have allusion made to both of the promises made to Abraham, both of them being introduced and reiterated to Isaac; but that is no proof that they are one. If you and I had lived neighbors twelve years ago, and had made two contracts, one to run ten years and the other fifteen, or any other time, we might meet to-day and talk about the two contracts in one and the same breath, and that would not prove them to be one and the same. Nor does the fact that we find the two separate and distinct promises made to Abraham spoken of in the same verse of the Bible, prove that those two promises are one and the same.

Let us now go one step further. Turn to Genesis, 28th chapter, 12th and 14th verses inclusive:

"And he dreamed, and behold a ladder set up on the earth, and the top of it reached to heaven; and behold the angels of God ascending and descending on it. And, behold, the Lord stood above it and said, I am the Lord God of Abraham thy father, and the God of Isaac: the land whereon thou liest, to thee will I give it, and to thy seed; And thy seed shall be as the dust of the earth; and thou shall spread abroad to the west, and to the east, and to the north, and to the south: and in the and in thy seed shall all the families of the earth be blessed."

Here, likewise, both of the promises made to Abraham are repeated. Observe, however, that while here in one place, where reference is made to a temporal inheritance, the word "seed" is used, plural, meaning multiplicity of individuals; whilst in the other place, where the promise of the Messiah is alluded to, it is "seed," singular. This is the true sense of the original.

Mark in the next place that the first promise recorded in Genesis 12th chapter, was made to Abraham in the 76th year of his age—the other in the 99th year of his age—

there being therefore 23 years difference in the date of these two transactions. Not only this, but there are also different matters embodied in the two which furnishes still another evidence of the fact that the two promises are wholly distinct one from the other. One was a promise of the whole land of Palestine, the other was a promise that through Abraham and his seed should all the families of the earth be blessed. One was connected with the ordinance of circumcision—the other had no reference to it. The meaning of one was limited by and confined to something called "nation" (and by and by we find out what it is,) while the other asserts that nations should come from him.

Go with me now to Galatians 3d chapter, 8th and 9th verses.

"And the scripture, forseeing that God would justify the heathen through faith, preached before the gospel unto Abraham, saying, In thee shall all nations be blessed. So then they which be of faith are blessed with faithful Abraham."

Here we find that that which is called "the gospel preached to Abraham," was the identical thing recorded in the 12th chapter of Genesis. Mark this passage. Not a word is said about the promise of a temporal inheritance—not a word about a farm—not a word about the land of Palestine; but the one great thought towers above all others in this passage—the thought of the spiritual promise made to Abraham: "In thee and in thy seed shall all the nations of the earth be blessed."

Look, if you please, at the Acts of the Apostles, 13th chapter, 32d and 33d verses:

"And we declare unto you glad tidings, how that the promise which was made unto the fathers, God hath fulfilled the same unto us their children, in that he hath raised up Jesus again; as it is also written in the second psalm, Thou art my Son, this day have I begotten thee."

What have we here? Simply this thought—that the very promise God made unto the fathers he had fulfilled in the resurrection of his Son from the dead. Keep before your minds the radical difference there is between the two promises, in whatever point of view we contemplate them; and not only so, but observe also that here we have one of those promises fulfilled. So says the unerring voice of Inspiration. But read on a little further in this same place:

"And as concerning that he raised him up from the dead, now no more to return to corruption, he said on this wise, I will give you the sure mercies of David. Wherefore he saith also in another psalm, Thou shalt not suffer thine Holy One to see corruption. For David, after he had served his own generation by the will of God, fell on sleep, and was laid unto his fathers, and saw corruption: But he, whom God raised again, saw no corruption.

"Be it known unto you therefore, men and brethren, that through this man is preached unto you the forgiveness of sins:"

Here we have in the most positive terms the declaration of the fulfillment of the promise made in Genesis, 12th chapter, in the resurrection of God's Son from the dead.

We now call attention to Galatians, 3d chapter, 16th and 19th verses, inclusive:

"Now to Abraham and his seed were the promises made. He saith not, And to seeds, as of many; but as of one, And to thy seed, which is Christ. And this I say, That the covenant that was confirmed before of God in Christ, the law, which was four hundred and thirty years after, cannot disannul, that it should make the promise of none effect. For if the inheritance be of the law, it is no more of the promise: but God gave it to Abraham by promise. Wherefore then serveth the law? It was added because of transgressions, till the seed should come to whom the promise was made; and it was ordained by angels in the hand of a mediator."

Here we have this great promise made to Abraham, that "in his seed should all the nations of the earth be blessed," confined and bound down by the voice of the Eternal himself to one single individual, the Lord Jesus

Christ. Take this in connection with the 8th and 9th verses:

"And the scripture, foreseeing that God would justify the heathen through faith, preached before the gospel unto Abraham, saying, In thee shall all nations be blessed. So then they which be of faith are blessed with faithful Abraham."

This same chapter informs us what the blessing of Abraham is, for we are told in the 9th verse that "they which be of faith are blessed with faithful Abraham." And again, in the 14th verse, "That the blessing of Abraham might come upon the Gentiles through Jesus Christ, that we might receive the promise of the spirit through faith." Read the 16th and 20th verses, inclusive:

"Now to Abraham and his seed were the promises made. He saith not, And to seeds, as of many; but as of one, And to thy seed, which is Christ. And this I say, That the covenant that was confirmed before of God in Christ, the law, which was four hundred and thirty years after, cannot disannul, that it should make the promise of none effect. For if the inheritance be of the law, it is no more of the promise: but God gave it to Abraham by promise. Wherefore then serveth the law? It was added because of transgressions, till the seed should come to whom the promise was made; and it was ordained by angels in the hand of a mediator. Now, a mediator is not a mediator of one; but God is one."

Pass on now to the 22d verse:

"But the scripture hath concluded all under sin, that the promise by faith of Jesus Christ might be given to them that believe."

Here we have the promise confined exclusively to believers. Read on still further:

"But before faith came, we were kept under the law, shut up unto the faith which should afterwards be revealed. Wherefore the law was our school-master to bring us unto Christ, that we might be justified by faith. But after that faith is come, we are no longer under a school-master. For ye are all the children of God by faith in Christ Jesus. For as many of you as have been baptized into Christ, have put on Christ. There is neither Jew nor Greek, there is neither bond nor free, there is neither male nor female: for ye are all one in Christ Jesus. And if ye be Christ's, then are ye Abraham's seed, and heirs according to the promise."

Mark that the Apostle, throughout all of this sublime argument, is talking about the one promise embodied in these words: "In thee and in thy seed shall all the families of the earth be blessed." He has declared this promise to be of a spiritual character—this blessing to be of a spiritual, and not of a fleshly nature. In short, he shows us clearly and indisputably that it is no more and no less than justification by faith.

Look, if you please, upon the other hand; and every time that you find the covenant of circumcision mentioned, the idea of the possession of the land of Palestine, as a temporal inheritance, is closely connected with it; whereas, we have seen that whenever the other promise is spoken of, it is connected by the context with the idea of spiritual blessing.

Let me here call your attention to one other very important question. Has the promise of the Eternal that Abraham's seed should possess the land of Palestine, been positively fulfilled or not? Just upon this point much of this important issue turns. We call your attention to the proof that every word of this promise has positively been fulfilled in times long past. Turn to Joshua, 24th chapter, 13th verse:

"And I have given you a land for which ye did not labor, and cities which ye built not, and ye dwell in them; of the vineyards and olive-yards which ye planted not do ye eat."

Take this in connection with the 23d chapter and 13th verse:

"Know for a certainty that the Lord your God will no more drive out any of these nations from before you: but they shall be snares and traps unto you, and scourges in your sides, and thorns in your eyes, until ye perish from off this good land which the Lord your God hath given you."

Here we may with perfect confidence rest this question on the testimony of these two witnesses. My first witness says positively that the Lord has given them the land for which they did not labor, and has so given it to them that they positively have possession of it. And that is not all. He tells them, moreover, that the Lord has given them cities which they builded not, and they dwelt in them, and that they ate of oliveyards and vineyards, which they planted not.

Notice the language of my first witness, found in the 14th verse of the preceding chapter. It is the language of Joshua, who took Moses' place and led the Hebrews into Palestine, the land promised by the Eternal to their fathers. In his dying address to the people he says: "Ye know in all your hearts and in all your souls." Could language more forcible be used by any human being? Know what? "That not one thing hath failed of all the good things which the Lord your God spoke concerning you—*all* are come to pass unto you, and not one thing hath failed thereof." Mark the word "*all*." "*All* are come to pass." Here, then, we are reduced to this dilemma: either Joshua is a false witness, or that promise made to Abraham in the covenant of circumcision was entirely fulfilled to the letter. The land was given to them, and thus God's veracity stands unimpeachable forever, although the Hebrew nation, after entering into the enjoyment of their promised possessions, may, by a breach of their covenant, have expatriated themselves and been everlastingly driven therefrom. The promise of Jehovah's had been fulfilled to the very letter.

We have, then, first the wide contrast there is between the two promises—the one embodying the Messiah, the other embodying the promise of the land of Palestine, the latter of which Joshua declares to have been already fulfilled to the very letter. He says that not one jot nor one tittle of all the promises has been left unredeemed. And hence, as a natural consequence, there is nothing left to be redeemed in the future. If the Hebrew race has forfeited its inheritance, that is their own fault, and they must eat the fruit of their own doings.

One thought more, and that is this: There is not a solitary promise of the restoration of the old house of Israel, from the beginning of the Word of God to the end, but was made prior to their return from the Babylonish captivity, and found its fulfilment in that return and restoration. Not one of Israel's old prophets ever uttered a prediction concerning the return of the Hebrew nation on this side, in point of time, of the rebuilding of Jerusalem and her temple, under the edict of Cyrus, and confirmed after his death by his successor. And this one fact tells more than volumes, upon this important question before us at this time. It is an index pointing, with the the unerring certainty of absolute truth, to the one great idea, that these promises, one and all, had a reference to the coming up of that people out of Babylon, and that they, one and all, found their complete and entire fulfilment there. From that time on, there is no promise whatever that the literal house of Israel will ever be returned again to their own land. Thus throwing in a most positive denial right here that from that time on any promise whatever was made that the literal house of Israel would ever be returned to their own land. In our next speech we shall show reasons therefor. For in making this declaration we know whereof we affirm.

---

## NEG.—J. M. STEPHENSON.—FIFTH SPEECH.

The first point that I shall notice in my opponent's argument has reference to Abraham and his seed having an everlasting inheritance in the land of Canaan. I will take no issue with him, however, until I have read the 17th chapter of Genesis, and 7th and 8th verses: "And I will establish my covenant between me and thee and thy seed after thee in their generations, for an everlasting covenant, to be a God unto thee and to thy seed after thee. And I will give unto thee, and to thy seed after thee, the land wherein thou art a stranger, all the land of Canaan, for an everlasting possession; and I will be their God." My opponent says the covenant here alluded to had no reference whatever to a landed estate. Let us turn and read the 18th verse of the 15th chapter of Genesis, where it is first mentioned, and see whether that be true or not: "In the same day the Lord made a covenant with Abram, saying, Unto thy seed have I given this land, from the river of Egypt unto the great river Euphrates." "And the Lord said unto Abram, after that Lot was separated from him, Lift up now thine eyes, and look from the place where thou art northward, and southward, and eastward, and westward; for all the land which thou seest, to thee will I give it, and to thy seed forever." Genesis xiii: 14, 15. When God made this covenant with Abraham, he said he would give him "this land;" and if Mr. Russell's position is true, then the Almighty must have made a great mistake. Whom shall we believe, Mr. Russell or the great God? Judge ye.

Let us now see whether the covenant alluded to in the 17th chapter of Genesis included land or not. Read the 8th verse of that chapter: "And I will give unto thee, and to thy seed after thee, the land wherein thou art a stranger, all the land of Canaan, for an everlasting possession; and I will be their God." My opponent says that the promise related to the covenant of circumcision. In the proof text that he quoted from the 26th chapter of Genesis, nothing is said about circumcision. In the long talk with Jacob, in the 28th chapter of Genesis, nothing is said about circumcision. In the 3d verse of the 26th chapter the Lord tells Isaac that he will "perform the oath" which he sware unto Abraham, his father. And in the 5th verse he gives the reason why he was going to give to Isaac and Abraham's seed the land of Canaan, in these words: "Because that Abraham obeyed my voice and kept my charge, my commandments, my statutes, and my laws." That was why the Lord was going to do all this for Abraham's seed. Nothing is said about circumcision. The Almighty said to Jacob: "The land whereon thou liest, to thee will I give it, and to thy seed. And thy seed shall be as the dust of the earth; and thou shalt spread abroad to the west, and to the east, and to the north, and to the south; and in thee and in thy seed shall all the families of the earth be blessed. And, behold, I am with thee, and will keep thee in all places whither thou goest, and will bring thee again into this land; for I will not leave thee, until I have done that which I have spoken to thee of." Genesis xxviii: 14, 15. You see that my friend Russell's own witnesses are against him. Nothing is said here except about a landed estate. If this evidence is not enough to make out a valid title to land, then it is impossible to make a valid deed of conveyance.

While we are in the Old Testament, I will call attention to the proofs by which my opponent seeks to show the fulfilment of these promises in times past. Turn to Joshua, 24th chapter, 18th verse—which is one of the texts he quoted:

"And I have given you a land for which ye did not labor, and cities which ye built not, and ye dwell in them; of the vineyards and olive-yards which ye planted not do ye eat."

Here nothing is said about the fulfillment of any promise made to Abraham or to Isaac or to Jacob; but he also quotes from the 24th chapter and 14th and 15th verses.

' Now therefore fear the Lord, and serve him in sincerity and in truth; and put away the gods which your fathers served on the other side of the flood, and in Egypt; and serve ye the Lord. And if it seem evil unto you to serve the Lord, choose ye this day whom ye will serve; whether the gods which your fathers served that were on the other side of the flood, or the Gods of the Amorites, in whose land ye dwell; but as for me and my house, we will serve the Lord."

His second witness contradicts his first, if we adopt

his explanation of the meaning of these passages of scripture. His second witness controverts the very points which he is trying to establish. Does it follow that because the Lord God had brought the children of Israel up out of the land of Egypt, and had given them cities which they builded not, and vineyards which they planted not, and had made them to possess the gates of their enemies, that therefore he had already fulfilled all his promises made to Abraham, Isaac and Jacob? The very passage of scripture last adduced by my opponent shows that ho had not. He proved that in case of their disobedience the Lord would drive them out of that land. It was not yet given to them for an everlasting inheritance. The promise of God to Abraham was not yet fulfilled. To prove that the children of Israel temporarily possessed the land, and to prove that that land was given to them as an everlasting inheritance are two wholly distinct and different things. He had proven one and that one we have always been ready to admit, but the other he has not proven nor can he.

I was somewhat amused at one point by my opponent's ingenuity; why did he when reading from the 3d chapter of Galatians, leave off at the 16th verse? He said there was no landed estate expressed in the allusion here made to the promise made to Abraham. It is admitted; but let us see if God will fulfill his promises or not. We have seen that he stands pledged to give to Abraham and his seed an *everlasting* possession in the land. He could not have given them that "everlasting" inheritance in time past. That is out of the question. To give that everlasting inheritance which he has promised will require the endless ages of eternity.

I will call your attention now to a text adduced by my opponent, viz: the last two verses of the 3d chapter of Acts.

"Ye are the children of the prophets, and of the covenant which God made with our fathers, saying unto Abraham, And in thy seed shall all the kindreds of the earth be blessed. Unto you first, God, having raised up his Son

Jesus, sent him to bless you, in turning away every one of you from his iniquities."

It does not follow that because these persons addressed by Peter were the children of Abraham, Isaac and Jacob, that therefore the blessing they were experiencing was the fulfillment of the promises made to Abraham that their seed should inherit the land forever. There is no connection between the two—God does not say he has fulfilled those promises—and he has not. The question therefore stands thus—will God fulfill his promise made to Abraham? If not then the Great God of truth will prove false to his word—unless he shall yet give to Abraham's seed an everlasting inheritance in the land of Palestine.

I will now notice the 7th chapter of the Acts of the Apostles, contained in the dying testimony of Stephen. Stephen in his defense before the Jewish tribunal, gives an account of God's dealings with Abraham and his posterity. What does he say in the 4th verse?

"Then came he (Abraham) out of the land of the Chaldeans, and dwelt in Charran; and from thence, when his father was dead, he removed him into this land, wherein ye now dwell."

Observe the language, "this land wherein ye now dwell." Read on—"And he gave him none inheritance in it, not so much as to set his foot on; yet he promised that he would give it to him for a possession, and to his seed after him, when as yet he had no child."

If Stephen does not here teach us that the promise made by God to Abraham was that of a landed estate, what language could convey such an idea? He says God brought Abraham into this land and he gave him *none* inheritance in it; yet he promised that he would give it to him and his seed. Thus teaching that the promise had not been fulfilled. God did not give to Abraham or to his seed an everlasting possession of that land; yet he promised that he would do so. Stephen meant by the language he used, one of two things — either he meant that God had made to Abraham a promise that he never intended to perform, or else he understood that that promise was yet to be performed in the future.

Turn now to Hebrews 11th chapter and 8th verse. Here Paul in tracing the origin of the Gospel, goes back to God's call to Abraham.

"By faith Abraham, when he was called to go out into a place which he should after receive for an inheritance, obeyed; and he went out, not knowing whither he went."

In the next verse we are told that Abraham dwelt in tabernacles with Isaac and Jacob, the heirs with him of the same promise. Here he brings them out into the land of promise. Paul calls it the land of Promise.

"By faith he sojourned in the land of promise, as in a strange country, dwelling in tabernacles with Isaac and Jacob, the heirs with him of the same promise."

A land of promise is one thing and a land of possession is quite another. Abraham dwelt with Isaac and Jacob, the heirs with him of the same promise. An heir is not a possessor but an expectant of a future possession. And they all died in faith, not having received the promised possession.

Did Abraham Isaac and Jacob receive their possession before they died? Read the 13th verse of this same chapter, and on, including the 16th.

"These all died in faith, not having received the promises, but having seen them afar off, and were persuaded of them, and embraced them, and confessed that they were strangers and pilgrims on the earth. For they that say such things declare plainly that they seek a country. And truly if they had been mindful of that country from whence they came out, they might have had opportunity to have returned. But now they desire a better country, that is, an heavenly; wherefore God is not ashamed to be called their God; for he hath prepared for them a city."

I will now call your attention to the continuation of the subject where I left it on Saturday. The first point to which I invite your attention is the next essential element of the kingdom. I have proved to you that in the kingdom of God there will be found to exist, at least four of the essential elements of all kingdoms—first a king—second, a royal cabinet, (composed of the saints of the Most High,) third, a territory (viz. the land of Canaan from the river of Egypt to the great river of Euphrates,) and fourth, subjects, (namely the literal twelve tribes of Israel restored.)

I now propose to demonstrate that the kingdom of God will have another element of all kingdoms that have ever existed upon earth; namely, a metropolis. Turn if you please to the 2d chapter of Isaiah, and 4th chapter of Micah, where you will find Jerusalem presented to us as the metropolitan city of the kingdom of God. In the 4th chapter of Micah, and the first verse we find this language.

"But in the last days it shall come to pass, that the mountain of the house of the Lord shall be established in the top of the mountains, and it shall be exalted above the hills; and people shall flow unto it. And many nations shall come, and say, Come let us go up to the mountain of the Lord, and to the house of the God of Jacob; and he will teach us of his ways, and we will walk in his paths; for the law shall go forth of Zion, and the word of the Lord from Jerusalem."

My opponent has saved me the trouble of proving that the passages immediately preceding this prediction, has reference to the destruction of Jerusalem by the Romans thirty-eight years and more after the day of Pentecost.

Having followed the narrative down to that point, the prophet then launches forth into the future, and tells us what shall come to pass "in the last days." It will not do to speak of this kingdom in connection with the day of Pentecost, for the prophet had already traced the history of the Jewish nation down to the time when the Roman ploughshares were driven over the foundations of the temple, thirty-eight years after the day of Pentecost, and then, using the future tense and speaking of things yet to come to pass, he tells us what shall come to pass in the last days. In like manner, Isaiah speaks of the establishment of the kingdom in the last days:

"The word that Isaiah the son of Amos saw concerning Judah and Jerusalem. And it shall come to pass in the last days, that the mountain of the Lord's house shall be established in the top of the mountains, and shall be exalted above the hills; and all nations shall flow unto it."

Unless you can make the future tense mean the past tense, you must understand the words "last days," to have reference not to the destruction of Jerusalem, but to the last days of the dispensation in which we live. Jerusalem upon Mount Zion is to be the metropolitan city of the world. Thus, and thus only, can Jerusalem be established in the top of Mount Zion, and thus only can all nations flow unto it.

I will ask my opponent this plain question—was this the case on the day of Pentecost? Did all nations flow unto the mountain of the Lord's house on the day of Pentecost? To be sure we are told that there were present at Jerusalem on the day of Pentecost, men out of every nation under heaven; but *a few men out of every nation* and *all nations* are widely different things. Did they beat their swords into ploughshares and their spears into pruning hooks? and did the nations learn war no more? All this was to take place at the time mentioned by the prophet, and unless my opponent can make it appear that all this was actually fulfilled on the day of Pentecost, then there is not the slightest possible reason to fix the establishment of the Kingdom of God upon that day.

Again, I refer you to the language of our Savior: "Swear not at all; neither by Heaven, for it is God's throne; nor by the earth, for it is his footstool; nor by Jerusalem, for it is *the city of the Great King*."

Turn, now, to Revelations, 21st and 22d. And just here I desire to meet another objection. My opponent tells us that the holy city, the New Jerusalem, that John saw come down from God out of Heaven, and that it was in Heaven before it came down. In reply to this, I would point him to the 12th chapter, where we find that the great dragon is spoken of as being in Heaven; and to the

13th chapter, where the beast with seven heads and ten horns is also represented as being in Heaven. The woman clothed with the sun, and the moon under her feet, was represented as being in Heaven, and so, likewise, was Christ sitting upon his white horse, followed by the hosts of Heaven, and making war upon the beast, the false prophet and the kings of the earth, who are also represented as being in Heaven. Now, will my opponent have us believe that these great beasts and dragons are to be transplanted beyond the starry skies, where God and his angels are? It is evident at first glance that such is not the fact. This is a figurative representation of what was to take place upon the earth, and is not to be understood as taking place in Heaven. Let us turn now, to the 21st chapter of Revelations, and there we find another figurative representation of what is to take place upon the earth—of a city that is to be built upon the earth—and we are told that "the nations of them that are saved shall walk in the light of it, and the kings of the earth bring their glory and honor into it." Are these nations of the earth to scale the walls of Heaven in order to bring their glory and honor into the city of the Great King? But turn again to the 13th, 14th and 15th verses of the 22d chapter:

"I am Alpha and Omega, the beginning and the end, the first and the last. Blessed are they that do his commandments, that they may have right to the tree of life, and may enter in through the gates into the city. For without are dogs, and sorcerers, and whoremongers, and murderers, and idolaters, and whosoever loveth and maketh a lie."

Here we find that while Christ and his saints are within the walls of this grand metropolitan city of the Great King, without are the nations of the earth with all their wickedness, their superstitions, their idolatry and their abominations. We learn moreover, from the same passage, that those nations are yet in a mortal state, that they are diseased, and that there is within the city a remedy for all their diseases, (verse 1, chapter 22,) and that to this remedy the obedient among the nations shall have access, while the rebellious and disobedient are left without to perish in their sins.

In the next place the Kingdom of God, in common with all other kingdoms, will have a law. In the language of the Lord's prayer, we find a recognition of the great truth that the will of God will be the supreme law of the world. "Thy kingdom come, thy *will* be done on earth as it is done in Heaven." The *will* of God, therefore, is to be the supreme law of the Kingdom of God. We find the same truth presented in the 14th verse of the 22d chapter of Revelations: "Blessed are they who keep his commandments, that they may have right to the tree of life, and may enter in through the gates into the city."

See, also, Isaiah, 2d chapter, 1st to 5th verses.

I have now proved that the Kingdom of God will possess the six essential elements of all kingdoms, namely: a king, subjects, a territory, a royal cabinet, a capital and a law; in fact, everything that belongs to a perfect kingdom. In all these respects, therefore, we may take the declarations of the word of God as refering to a literal kingdom to be establised on the earth.

The next point that naturally presents itself to our minds is the time when this Kingdom of God shall be established. We have examined fully the nature of this Kingdom, and from the beginning of Genesis to the end of Revelations we have found nothing in the word of God that does not point clearly and unmistakeably to a literal kingdom, a literal king, a literal metropolis, a literal reign of the Lord Jesus Christ upon the earth, as King of Kings and Lord of Lords. You might as well attempt to snatch the sun from the solar system as to attempt to erase from the declarations and promises of God's word the great central idea that runs through them all, of the establishment, in the future, of God's Kingdom on the earth, and the bringing back of this revolted world in allegiance to God.

Is this, then, a future, or is it a past event? I affirm that the kingdom promised to Jesus Christ by all the prophets, is a future event in this world's history. The first two witnesses that I shall bring before you in support of this position, are the prophets of God—Isaiah and Micah—who predicted, under prophetic inspiration, the establishment of the kingdom of God in a period of time called by them "the last days," which period of time was still future at the time of the destruction of Jerusalem.

"The word that Isaiah the son of Amoz saw concerning Judah and Jerusalem. And it shall come to pass in the last days, that the mountain of the Lord's house shall be established in the top of the mountains, and shall be exalted above the hills; and all nations shall flow unto it. And many people shall go and say, Come ye, and let us go up to the mountain of the Lord, to the house of the God of Jacob; and he will teach us of his ways, and we will walk in his paths: for out of Zion shall go forth the law, and the word of the Lord from Jerusalem. And he shall judge among the nations, and shall rebuke many people: and they shall beat their swords into ploughshares, and their spears into pruning-hooks: nation shall not lift up sword against nation, neither shall they learn war any more.

"O house of Jacob, come ye, and let us walk in the light of the Lord.

"But in the last days it shall come to pass, that the mountain of the house of the Lord shall be established in the top of the mountains, and it shall be exalted above the hills; and people shall flow unto it. And many nations shall come, and say, Come, and let us go up to the mountain of the Lord, and to the house of the God of Jacob; and he will teach us of his ways, and we will walk in his paths: for the law shall go forth of Zion, and the word of the Lord from Jerusalem.

"And he shall judge among many people, and rebuke strong nations afar off; and they shall beat their swords into plough-shares, and their spears into pruning-hooks: nation shall not lift up sword against nation, neither shall they learn war any more. But they shall sit every man under his vine and under his fig-tree; and none shall make them afraid: for the mouth of the Lord of hosts hath spoken it."

The next testimony I shall advance is that of our Lord Jesus Christ, recorded in the 19th chapter of Matthew, and 28th verse:

"And Jesus said unto them, Verily I say unto you, that ye which have followed me, in the regeneration when the Son of man shall sit in the throne of his glory, ye also shall sit upon twelve thrones, judging the twelve tribes of Israel."

You have been told by my opponent that Christ is even now upon HIS throne; but I propose to prove to you the opposite. Turn with me to Revelations, 3d chapter and 21st verse:

"To him that overcometh will I grant to sit with me in my throne, even as I also overcame, and am set down with my Father in his throne."

When will Christ receive his own throne? Turn with me to Matthew, 25th chapter and 31st verse:

"When the Son of man shall come in his glory, and all the holy angels with him, then shall he sit upon the throne of his glory."

Notice the force of the adverb of time, "then." THEN shall He sit upon the throne of HIS glory, when he shall come in his glory, and all the holy angels with him.

## AFF.—P. T. RUSSELL.—SIXTH SPEECH.

I shall take up the thread of my argument at the point I had reached when I closed. We had found, in the first place, that the Hebrew nations had broken the covenant, and secondly, that in consequence thereof, they had expatriated themselves and had forfeited all right and title to the things promised in Genesis, 17th chapter. And here also we found the reason why Paul, in Hebrews, 8th chapter and 9th verse, represents the Lord as saying, "Because they continued not in my covenant, and I regarded them not."

In connection with this language, let us take Matthew, 21st chapter, 38th and 41st verses, inclusive:

"But when the husbandman saw the son, they said among themselves, This is the heir; come, let us kill him, and let us seize on his inheritance. And they caught him, and cast him out of the vineyard, and slew him. When the lord therefore of the vineyard cometh, what will he do unto those husbandmen? They say unto him, He will miserably destroy those wicked men, and will let out his vineyard unto other husbandmen, which shall render him the fruits in their seasons."

One point I wish to fasten here, and that is this: that God's protection and government should be taken away from literal Israel because of their murdering his son, and should be given to another nation. Now if it was thus to be taken from literal Israel, after the flesh, and given to another nation which should render to the Lord their fruits in season, could the Jews—the nation of Israel after that thing was taken from it and given to another nation—be said truly to have it any longer? If I or the gentleman who has just preceded me, should say to one of you, "I will take away a certain thing from you and give it to another person who will do justice to it," I ask what would be the idea from that language? Would the idea be that you were any longer to have the possession of that thing, or would it be that another person should possess it? The fact of their becoming the murderers of the only begotten Son of God, furnished an all-sufficient reason for God's government and protection being taken away from them and being given to another nation which will render to him the fruits in their season.

Go with me now to Jeremiah, 18th chapter, where we have an illustration of this important matter from the mouth of God himself. Read the first seventeen verses of that chapter:

"The word which came to Jeremiah from the Lord, saying, Arise, and go down to the potter's house, and there I will cause thee to hear my words.

"Then I went down to the potter's house, and, behold, he wrought a work on the wheels. And the vessel that he made of clay was marred in the hand of the potter: so he made it again another vessel, as seemed good to the potter to make it. Then the word of the Lord came to me, saying, O house of Israel, cannot I do with you as this potter? saith the Lord. Behold, as the clay is in the potter's hand, so are ye in mine hand, O house of Israel.

"At what instant I shall speak concerning a nation, and concerning a kingdom, to pluck up, and to pull down, and to destroy it; If that nation, against whom I have pronounced, turn from their evil, I will repent of the evil that I thought to do unto them. And at what instant I shall speak concerning a nation, and concerning a kingdom, to build and to plant it; if it do evil in my sight, that it obey not my voice, then I will repent of the good, wherewith I said I would benefit them.

"Now therefore go to, speak to the men of Judah, and to the inhabitants of Jerusalem, saying, Thus saith the Lord; Behold, I frame evil against you, and devise a device against you: return ye now every one from his evil way, and make your ways and your doings good. And they said, There is no hope: but we will walk after our own devices, and we will every one do the imagination of his evil heart. Therefore thus saith the Lord; Ask ye now among the heathen, who hath heard such things: the virgin of Israel hath done a very horrible thing.

"Will a man leave the snow of Lebanon which cometh from the rock of the field? or shall the cold flowing waters that come from another place be forsaken? Because my people hath forgotten me, they have burned incense to vanity, and they have caused them to stumble in their ways from the ancient paths, to walk in paths, in a way not cast up; to make their land desolate, and a perpetual hissing; every one that passeth thereby shall be astonished, and wag his head. I will scatter them as with an east wind before the enemy; I will shew them the back, and not the face, in the day of their calamity."

Just here I ask this plain question: If in the time of their calamity He is going to show them the back and not the face, where will you find the time when He shall turn his face to them again? You may go over all the face of the earth, search every land under the broad arch of Heaven, and wherever you find one solitary individual of the Hebrew race, he will tell you "This is the day of our calamity." Just so long as the Hebrew race are dispersed abroad upon the face of the earth, it will be the day of their calamity, a sure indication of the perpetuity of God's judgments because of their iniquity.

An important principle is involved just here, in this language, found in the 9th and 10th verses of this same chapter:

"And at what instant I shall speak concerning a nation, and concerning a kingdom, to build and to plant it; if it do evil in my sight, that it obey not my voice, then I will repent of the good, wherewith I said I would benefit them."

These words in their import span the entire arch of all time, and show clearly and in a strong light the simple truth, that if man, after entering into a covenant with his Maker, breaks that covenant, that breach brings his right to all the privileges and advantages growing out of that covenant to a perpetual end.

In perfect keeping with this idea, you will find the language of Paul, in Romans, 9th chapter, where the Apostle is arguing the great thought of the rejection of the old house of Israel. In the 21st verse he calls up the very same idea expressed by Jeremiah in the 18th chapter of his prophecy, clothed in similar language, and making use of the identical figure there employed:

"Hath not the potter power over the clay, of the same lump to make one vessel unto honor, and another unto dishonor? What if God, willing to shew his wrath, and to make his power known, endured with much longsuffering the vessels of wrath fitted to destruction: And that he might make known the riches of his glory on the vessels of mercy, which he had afore prepared unto glory. Even us, whom he hath called, not of the Jews only, but also of the Gentiles?"

In perfect keeping with this you will find the language of the Lord of Hosts, addressed to ancient Israel, as recorded in Ezekiel, 16th chapter, 44th and succeeding verses. Go with me, and let us learn a lesson of truth from the lips of the ancient prophet. He is addressing ancient Israel:

"Behold, every one that useth proverbs shall use this proverb against thee, saying, As is the mother so is her daughter. Thou art thy mother's daughter, that loatheth her husband and her children; and thou art the sister of thy sisters, which loathed their husbands and their children: your mother was a Hittite, and your father an Amorite. And thine elder sister is Samaria, she and her daughters that dwell at thy left hand: and thy younger sister, that dwelleth at thy right hand, is Sodom and her daughters. Yet hast thou not walked after their ways, nor done after their abominations: but as if that were a very little thing, thou wast corrupted more than they in all thy ways. As I live, saith the Lord God, Sodom thy sister hath not done, she nor her daughters, as thou hast done, thou and thy daughters. Behold, this was the iniquity of thy sister Sodom, pride, fulness of bread, and abundance of idleness was in her and in her daughters, neither did she strengthen the hand of the poor and needy. And they were haughty, and committed abomination before me: therefore I took them away as I saw good. Neither hath Samaria committed half thy sins; but thou hast multiplied thine abominations more than they, and hast justified thy sisters in all thine abominations which thou hast done. Thou also, which hast judged thy sisters, bear thine own shame for thy sins that thou hast committed more abominable than they: they are more righteous than thou: yea, be thou confounded also, and bear thy shame, in that thou hast justified thy sisters."

Mark, now, the language of the following verses, 53d and 54th: "When I shall bring again their captivity, the captivity of Sodom and her daughters, and the captivity of Samaria and her daughters, then will I bring again the captivity of thy captives in the midst of them, that thou mayest bear thine own shame, and mayest be confounded in all that thou hast done, in that thou art a comfort unto them." Read on a little further: "When thy sisters, Sodom and her daughters, shall return to their former estate, and Samaria and her daughters shall return to their former estate, then thou and thy daughters shall return to your former estate; for thy sister Sodom was not mentioned by thy mouth in the day of thy pride." Ezekiel xvi: 55, 56.

Just here we pause to ask two or three questions. Upon the hypothesis that ancient Israel is to be literally restored, in what shape, and under what circumstances is she to come back? Right between Sodom, that ancient city of the plain, which was too polluted and vile to be suffered to remain upon the face of the earth by the Almighty, and ancient Samaria with all her pollutions. Sodom on Israel's right hand and Samaria on her left— like joined with like—with Sodom and Samaria as her right and left hand supporters—is ancient Israel to be restored. When Sodom, with her Sodomy, and Samaria, with her manifold iniquities upon her, shall be restored, then, and not till then, shall ancient Israel be restored.

The Lord God of heaven and earth once decided in his own mind that the ancient Sodomites were too vile and abominable to live, and hence, with the besom of destruction, he swept them from the face of the earth; and is he going to change his mind now, and bring them up again and restore them again to the places they once occupied among the nations of the earth? Their former estate was such a stench in the nostrils of the Eternal that he would not allow them even to exist upon his footstool. And yet, if he is not going to bring up the Sodomites and give them again a name and a place among the nations of the earth, no more is he going to restore Israel to her former position in their own land. And in perfect harmony with this view we find the language of Christ addressed to the old house of Israel, in Matthew, 23d chapter and 38th verse. In the preceding verse he tells them what would have been the case if they had been willing to hear and receive the truth; but they were disobedient and rejected the Messiah and his divine mission. And now what? Listen to the language of the 38th verse: But now "your house is left unto you desolate." And while thus we find this language of our Savior to be in perfect keeping with Ezekiel, 16th chapter, let us go to Malachi, the last chapter, and see what is there recorded. Read this chapter:

"For, behold, the day cometh that shall burn as an oven; and all the proud—yea, and all that do wickedly—shall be stubble; and the day that cometh shall burn them up, saith the Lord of hosts, that it shall leave them neither root nor branch.

"But unto you that fear my name shall the sun of righteousness arise with healing in his wings; and ye shall go forth and grow up as calves of the stall; and ye shall tread down the wicked; for they shall be ashes under the soles of your feet in the day that I shall do this, saith the Lord of hosts.

"Remember, ye, the law of Moses my servant, which I commanded unto him in Horeb for all Israel, with the statutes and judgments.

"Behold, I will send you Elijah, the prophet, before the coming of the great and dreadful day of the Lord. And he shall turn the heart of the fathers to the children, and the heart of the children to their fathers, lest I come and smite the earth with a curse."

This remarkable prophetic language found its fulfilment at the time of the destruction of Jerusalem and her temple by the Roman army commanded by Vespasian and his son Titus. Look, for a moment, at the language before us: "The day cometh that shall burn as an oven." Josephus, in his account of the destruction of Jerusalem, tells us that when the Romans had succeeded in effecting an entrance into the city, and had made themselves masters of all the rest of the city, the temple alone withstood their attacks, and there were gathered together an immense multitude of men, women and children. Beneath the temple were subterranean passages, and into these, when at last the Romans forced their way into the temple, the Jews crept by hundreds and by thousands. The Romans set the temple on fire. Titus, the Roman general, gave orders that the temple should be preserved; but a Roman soldier threw a firebrand into the building. It set fire to the structure, and so intense was the heat of the conflagration that followed that even the gold and silver that were about the temple were melted, and ran down into a pool; and these subterranean passages, into which the Jews were crowded by thousands upon thousands, were heated by the flames until they became indeed a very "oven." And thus was this remarkable prediction of the ancient prophet most signally fulfilled.

We are told by the prophet further, that the wicked should be ashes under the soles of the feet of the righteous in the day that the Lord should do this. After the fires that consumed the city and temple of Jerusalem had gone out, we are told by the historian that the ashes of these rebel Jews were lying scattered about upon the surface of the ground. And thus another portion of this remarkable prophecy found in the destruction of Jerusalem its full and complete fulfilment. Now, if the time when the righteous persons who are addressed in the language before us are to tread down the wicked, and when the wicked are ashes under their feet, is the time when Christ shall come again, as my opponent and his friends maintain, then the ashes of the wicked are to be taken up from the wreck of this dissolving earth as it passes away, and are to be scattered abroad over the face of the new earth; and in that view of the case, I think it will puzzle my opponent to tell where they are going to get scrapers enough, or who is to handle them.

The amount of the whole matter is simply this: The ancient Israelites have completely expatriated themselves by their wicked rebellion, and the Lord of hosts, in harmony with the language I have read, regards them not; and, regarding them not, as a natural consequence they are not those who are to inherit the kingdom concerning which we are now in controversy.

Let us contemplate, for a moment, the idea of the identity of the twelve tribes. I ask, in the apostolic writings and wherever they speak of Israel and of themselves as belonging to it, do they mean the literal Israel? or do they mean something else? Let us examine this question. Go with me to James, 1st chapter, 1st and 2d verses: "James, a servant of God and of the Lord Jesus Christ, to the twelve tribes which are scattered abroad, greeting. My brethren, count it all joy when ye fall into divers temptations."

Mark that James is here writing a letter to something, or to somebody, that he calls "the twelve tribes;" and, further, that the entire epistle, from the first word to the last, is evidently addressed to, and intended for, believers in Christ. All believers in the Lord Jesus Christ, therefore, are called "the twelve tribes." Now, unless literal Israel did, at the time this letter was written, believe in Christ, then something else is alluded to by James under the name of "the twelve tribes which are scattered abroad." What is that something? Go with me to the Acts of the Apostles, 26th chapter, and 6th and 7th verses: "And now I stand, and am judged for the hope of the promise made of God unto our fathers; unto which promise our twelve tribes, instantly serving God day and night, hope to come. For which hope's sake, King Agrippa, I am accused of the Jews." Here we have presented to us an important thought. Paul is speaking to what he calls "the twelve tribes," and who he says are "instantly serving God day and night." Were the twelve tribes of literal Israel serving God day and night when they clamored for the blood of our Lord and Savior Jesus Christ, crying, "Crucify him! crucify him! Away with him!" Were they serving God night and day when they were murdering the disciples and followers of the Savior? Were they serving God when they were doing despite to the spirit of grace? If they were not— and you and I know they were not—then one thing is certain, and that is, James and Paul called one thing the twelve tribes and my opponent calls another by that name. My opponent speaks of twelve tribes that certainly were not serving God, either by day or by night; and Paul spoke of "twelve tribes" who were "instantly serving God, day and night." And James speaks of the twelve tribes in a similar manner.

The position in which my opponent places himself just here is just about the same as that of a man who should call the rebel States of this nation the "Union," and "my policy" the law of the land. The tribes of whom my opponent speaks were just as much in rebellion at the time Paul wrote these words as ever were these rebel States against the authority of our own country. Can any one hesitate for a moment to answer the question whether at that time these rebel Jews were "serving God, day and night?" Who were the people who were "serving God, day and night?" You will find this people mentioned in the 9th chapter of Romans:

"What if God, willing to shew his wrath, and to make his power known, endured with much longsuffering the vessels of wrath fitted to destruction: and that he might make known the riches of his glory on the vessels of mercy, which he had afore prepared unto glory, even us, whom he hath called, not of the Jews only, but also of the Gentiles? As he saith also in Hosea, I will call them my people, which were not my people; and her beloved, which was not beloved."

In my next speech I will demonstrate that the word "people" is, in all such connections as that before us, a synonym of the word nation.

---

## NEG.—J. M. STEPHENSON—SIXTH SPEECH.

Before resuming the thread of my argument upon this question, I shall briefly and hastily sketch something like a reply to some of the positions assumed by my opponent.

He says that Israel is not to be restored until Sodom and Samaria shall be restored. Now, the Bible teaches us that the nations of the earth shall all be restored. Turn to the 22d Psalm and read the 27th verse:

"All the ends of the world shall remember and turn unto the Lord: and all the kindreds of the nations shall worship before thee."

Here the whole earth is spoken of as turning unto the Lord and worshiping before him. I accept, therefore, the issue tendered by my opponent upon this point.

I call attention, in the next place, to the issue he presents in reference to the restoration of Israel. Turn to the 37th chapter of Ezekiel, commencing with the 21st verse, and what have we here?

"And say unto them, thus saith the Lord God: Behold, I will take the children of Israel from among the heathen, whither they be gone, and will gather them on every side, and bring them into their own land: and I will make them one nation in the land upon the mountains of Israel; and one king shall be king to them all: and they shall be no more two nations, neither shall they be divided into two kingdoms any more at all: neither shall they defile themselves any more with their idols, nor with their detestable things, nor with any of their transgressions: but I will save them out of all their dwellingplaces, wherein they have sinned, and will cleanse them: so shall they be my people, and I will be their God."

The last rebel will be taken out of Israel before the Lord God shall acknowledge her again as his people. They shall be tried as gold is tried in the fire—all the rebellious and the disobedient are to be purged away, and as for the remainder, we are told in Ezekiel 37th chapter and 21st and following verses, that the children of Israel shall be gathered together upon the mountains of Israel and made into one nation, having one king, that they shall be cleansed, and that they shall be God's people and that he will be their God. Observe two or three points included in this prophecy: First, the two houses of Israel and Judah shall be united into one house, and the two nations into one nation, and they shall be planted together in the land, never again to be separated. In the next place, as to their condition. It is not to be spiritual, for God says he will gather them from among the heathen, whither they are gone, and bring them into their own land, and that he will cleanse them from their idols, and so on. Again, when Israel shall be thus gathered in on every side from among the nations, whither they had gone, and when they should be cleansed from their idolatry, they were to be greatly multiplied and increased—they were to have children and children's children, and God's covenant and his tabernacle were to be with them forever. All these circumstances go to show plainly that the reference to this future happy state of things that should come to pass was to a literal restoration of the literal kingdom of Israel, and not to a spiritual church.

The very same people that rejected Christ at his first advent will accept him at his second. God will grant them the spirit of grace, and they will say, "Blessed is he that cometh in the name of the Lord." Turn to the concluding verse of the 13th chapter of Luke, and read there what the Savior said in regard to his reception when he shall come again, by those who rejected and scorned him when he was upon the earth:

"Ye shall not see me until ye shall say, Blessed is he that cometh in the name of the Lord."

Turn again to the 11th chapter of Romans, and 15th verse:

"For if the casting away of them be the reconciling of the world, what shall the receiving of them be but life from the dead?"

Look again at the 25th verse of this same chapter, where the apostle says:

"For I would not, brethren, that ye should be ignorant of this mystery, lest ye should be wise in your own conceits; that blindness in part is happened to Israel, until the fulness of the Gentiles be come in."

Notice the use of the adverb "until" in this passage—an adverb that always limits a period of time past, and dates the beginning of a new epoch—"until" the fulness of the Gentiles be come in. Observe now the language of the next verse:

"And so all Israel shall be saved: as it is written, There shall come out of Sion the Deliverer, and shall turn away ungodliness from Jacob."

Go to the 14th Psalm and read the last verse:

"Oh, that the salvation of Israel were come out of Zion! When the Lord bringeth back the captivity of his people, Jacob shall rejoice, and Israel shall be glad."

My opponent referred to the first chapter of James and had something to say as to what James meant by the words, "twelve tribes." He also quoted from St. Paul to the same effect. Now, it is an undeniable truth that at that very time, before and since the twelve literal tribes of Israel were serving God day and night, after their ritual, a part used by synecdoche for the whole.

I now call your attention to the continuation of the subject where I left off. When my time expired I was in the very act of proving that the kingdom promised to Christ by all the prophets, would be established at his second advent, in connection with the resurrection of the dead; and the last text I quoted was one having reference to the coming of our Lord Jesus Christ in the glory of the Father, and with the holy angels; when, having been seated upon the throne of his glory, with all the nations standing in array before him, he separates the righteous from the wicked, and invites the blessed of the Father to come and inherit the kingdom prepared for them from the foundation of the world. Were all these things fulfilled on the day of Pentecost? Did Christ come on that day in the Glory of the Father and the holy angels? Did all nations stand before him? Was he then seated on the throne of this world? Were the righteous separated from the wicked then? Did he then invite the blessed of the Father to come and inherit the kingdom prepared for them from the foundation of the world? No. Go right back to the original charter of man's dominion, and you will find that the dominion and sovereignty of the whole earth is the dominion that was prepared for him. Did he receive the dominion and sovereignty of the whole earth on the day of Pentecost?

The next evidence that I shall bring in for the purpose of proving the futurity of the Kingdom of God, is the parable of the nobleman. Christ gave the Jews this parable, we are told, because they thought that the Kingdom of God should immediately appear. He was compelled to explain the position, and the relation he sustained to his kingdom in point of time. I will read from the 19th chapter of Luke. Christ, as you will observe, compares himself to a nobleman who went into a far country to receive a kingdom—to be invested with royalty, and to return:

"He said therefore, A certain nobleman went into a far county to receive for himself a kingdom and to return. And he called his ten servants, and delivered them ten pounds, and said unto them, Occupy till I come. But his citizens hated him, and sent a message after him, saying, We will not have this man to reign over us. And it came to pass that when he was returned, having received the kingdom, then he commanded these servants to be called unto him, to whom he had given the money, that he might know how much every man had gained by trading. Then came the first, saying, Lord, thy pound hath gained ten pounds. And he said unto him, Well, thou good servant: because thou hast been faithful in a very little, have thou authority over ten cities. And the second came, saying, Lord, thy pound hath gained five pounds. And he said likewise to him, Be thou also over five cities. And another came, saying, Lord, behold, here is thy pound, which I have kept laid up in a napkin: for I feared thee, because thou art an austere man: thou takest up that thou layedst not down, and reapest that thou didst not sow. And he saith unto him, Out of thine own mouth will I judge thee, thou wicked servant. Thou knewest that I was an austere man, taking up that I laid not down, and reaping that I did not sow: wherefore, then, gavest not thou my money into the bank, that at my coming I might have required mine own with usury. And he said unto them that stood by, Take from him the pound, and give it to him that hath ten pounds. (And they said unto him, Lord, he hath ten pounds.) For I say unto you, That unto every one which hath shall be given; and from him that hath not, even that he hath shall be taken away from him. But those mine enemies, which would not that I should reign over them, bring hither, and slay them before me."

Now that Christ referred in this parable to himself, is evident, first, from the fact that before the nobleman went away he divided his substance among his servants, and said to them, "Occupy till I come;" and secondly, from what his servants said of him, one class of them, "We will not have this man to reign over us." When the nobleman returned, he divided the emoluments among his faithful servants, and then said of the disloyal, "bring them here and slay them before me." It is apparent at a single glance, that the nobleman in the parable represented Christ. The Jews at that time were tributary to the Romans. Whenever a Roman conqueror would receive the dominion over any conquered province, he had to go to the palace of the Cezars, at Rome, and having there received his authority, he returned, and entered upon the administration of the affairs of government. Jesus was the nobleman, and the far country into which he went to receive a kingdom and return, was the court of his Father. He went up to Heaven to be invested with the dominion of all the earth, and to return from thence at his second advent. When he returns he is to receive the kingdom with the right to possess which he has been already clothed. It was when the nobleman returned that he entered upon his kingdom. When a Jewish nobleman went to Rome to be invested with authority, he did not go to reign there, at Rome; but he went to be invested with the right to reign on his return home, and then it was that he could be said to receive his kingdom, to be established upon his throne.

Listen now, to Paul's dying charge to his son Timothy. It begins thus:

"I charge thee therefore before God, and the Lord Jesus Christ, who shall judge the quick and the dead at his appearing and his kingdom."

When will Christ receive his kingdom? I answer, At the judgment of the quick and the dead.

Again, the truth that Christ will receive the kingdom at his second advent is evident, from the testimony of Peter and James, recorded in the 15th chapter of the Acts of the Apostles. James there is heard saying to the apostles and elders of the church:

"And after they had held their peace, James answered, saying, Men and brethren, hearken unto me. Simeon hath declared how God at the first did visit the Gentiles, to take out of them a people for his name. And to this agree the words of the prophets as it is written; after this I will return, and will build again the tabernacle of David which is fallen down, and I will build up again the ruins thereof, and I will set it up."

After having visited the Gentiles, and taken out of them a people for his name, he would return and build the tabernacle of David which had fallen down. Was the tabernacle rebuilt on the day of Pentecost? David never had but the one tabernacle, and that was the insignia of royal power. The *church*, at the time here referred to, was in ruins, and was to be rebuilt? Is that the idea? You cannot *rebuild* a thing that has not first been built and then afterwards been torn down.

Turn now to Revelations 11th chapter, beginning at the 15th verse.

"And the seventh angel sounded; and there were great voices in heaven, saying, The kingdoms of this world are become the kingdoms of our Lord, and of his Christ; and he shall reign for ever and ever. And the four and twenty elders, which sat before God on their seats, fell upon their faces, and worshiped God, saying, We give thee thanks, O Lord God Almighty, which art, and wast, and art to come; because thou hast taken to thee thy great power, and hast reigned. And the nations were angry, and thy wrath is come, and the time of the dead, that they should be judged, and that thou shouldest give reward unto thy servants the prophets, and to the saints, and them that fear thy name, small and great; and shouldest destroy them which destroy the earth."

We see here when Christ shall receive his kingdom. It will be when the seventh trumpet shall sound. I will let the angels of God preach to you to-day. When is it that they preach this great sermon which proclaims the conversion of the world, the judgment scene—the resurrection of the dead and the destruction of the earth's corrupters? When the seventh trumpet sounds—when is it that the kingdoms of this world become the kingdoms of our Lord and of his Christ? When the seventh trumpet sounds and the dead are brought up before the judgment seat, and are judged according to their works. Did the seventh trumpet sound on the day of Pentecost? Did the judgment of quick and dead take place on the day of Pentecost? Did God reward his servants the prophets, and them that fear his name, small and great, as he has promised to do on the day of Pentecost? Did the kingdoms of this world become the kingdom of our Lord and of his Christ on the day of Pentecost?

I have already brought forward abundant evidence to show that the time when Christ should receive his kingdom was not at the time of his first advent, nor at the time of his ascension, nor yet at the day of Pentecost; but that on the contrary it will be when God shall reward his servants and his prophets of old.

I now pause to notice the relation of Christ and his servants who shall reign with him, to their kingdom. What is the nature of Christ's possession of his kingdom? Is he a king *de facto*, or a king *de jure?* It is declared by Peter, in Acts 3d chapter and 15th verse, that they had crucified the Prince of Life, but that God had raised him from the dead. Again in the 5th chapter and 31st verse he represents Christ as being elevated to the right hand of God as a prince and a Savior, who should give repentance to Israel and remission of sins. He is called a prince. In Revelations 1st chapter, and 5th verse he is called the prince of the kings of the earth.

Turn now to Revelations 19th chapter and 16th verse, and you will find that at his second coming he shall come as a king. "King of Kings and Lord of Lords." Read the striking description here given in the 19th chapter of Revelations, of this glorious personage. He has on his head many crowns—his eyes were as a flame of fire—he was clothed in a vesture dipped in blood. Out of his mouth went a sharp sword, with which he should smite the nations, and he had upon his vesture and upon his thigh a name written — "King of Kings and Lord of Lords." Now Christ sustains to his future kingdom the relation of a prince, but when he shall come again he shall come in the splendor and glory of a king.

What relation did the saints of the Most High sustain on the day of Pentecost. I propose to show you that they possessed a kingdom in expectancy. Turn to the 8th chapter of Romans and you will there find what position Paul regarded himself and his brethren in Christ, as occupying at that time in relation to the kingdom of God. Read the 17th verse. "And if children, then heirs—heirs of God, and joint heirs with Christ." Being a joint heir with a prince makes a man also a prince. Had it been the law of the Russian Empire that two persons could reign at the same time, the Duke Constantine would have reigned along with the Emperor Nicholas—because he was his joint heir. That is precisely the idea of joint heirship. Turn now to the 5th verse of the 2d chapter of James.

"Hearken, my beloved brethren, Hath not God chosen the poor of this world rich in faith, and heirs of the kingdom which he hath promised to them that love him?"

Yes, my friends, to be an heir of the kingdom is to be a prince, and to be a prince is to be entitled to possess the throne and scepter when heirship shall be merged into possession.

Instead of the church being the kingdom all through

the writings of Christ and the Apostles, the kingdom is promised to the church as a reward—would it not be a strange thing if the church was promised to the church for a reward? The kingdom spoken of in the word of God, be its character whatever it may, is unquestionably held out to the church as an incentive to the acceptance of Christ. Now to offer to give a man that which he already possesses is no inducement—it is no incentive to him to do anything. They already had the church and hence there could be no propriety in holding out to them the promise of the church as an incentive. Hence it is clear that the kingdom promised was not the church. Said Christ to his disciples. "Fear not little flock for it is your Father's good pleasure to give you the *kingdom.*" My opponent will not argue that when Christ used that language, the disciples were in possession of what Christ promised to give them; but they were in possession of the church—therefore he could not have meant the church. The passage just quoted is in the 12th chapter of Luke, and at the 32d verse.

## AFF.—P. T. RUSSELL—SEVENTH SPEECH.

My opponent in one of his preceding speeches said that Christ is now filling out the type of the Aaronic order of priesthood, and that he will fill out the Melchizedekian order when he shall sit upon his throne. If Christ is now a priest after the order of Melchizedek, then he is now on his throne, and if he is now on his throne then now is the time of his kingdom. The issue as my opponent has placed it now, turns on this one point—is he or is he not now a priest after the order of Melchizedek? Here is the entire issue upon his own admission, for if Christ is now a priest after the order of Melchisedek, then he is now upon his throne, and if he is now on his throne then the time for him to occupy that throne, the time of his kingdom is now and not in the future. Having thus the issue clearly before us let us now turn to Hebrew 5th chapter, and 5th and 10th verses inclusive.

"So also Christ glorified not himself to be made a high priest; but he that said unto him, Thou art my Son, to-day have I begotten thee. As he saith also in another place, Thou art a priest for ever after the order of Melchisedek. Who in the days of his flesh, when he had offered up prayers and supplications with strong crying and tears unto him that was able to save him from death, and was heard in that he feared; Though he were a Son, yet learned he obedience by the things which he suffered; And being made perfect, he became the author of eternal salvation unto all them that obey him; Called of God a high priest after the order of Melchisedek."

Take in connection with this the 7th chapter of the same book and the 12th and 17th verses inclusive.

"For the priesthood being changed, there is made of necessity a change also of the law. For he of whom these things are spoken pertaineth to another tribe, of which no man gave attendance at the altar. For it is evident that our Lord sprang out of Judah; of which tribe Moses spake nothing concerning priesthood. And it is yet far more evident: for that after the similitude of Melchisedek there ariseth another priest, who is made, not after the law of a carnal commandment, but after the power of an endless life. For he testifieth, Thou art a priest forever after the order of Melchisedek."

Here we either have, in the language of the inspired Apostle, the climax of absurdity; or else, at the time he wrote these words Christ was an high priest after the order of Melchisedek; and if he was at that time an high priest after the order of Melchisedek, then was he at that very time upon his throne; and if he was then on his throne, he was also at that very time in possession of the promised kingdom. In other words, the kingdom spoken of by the prophet was established at least as early as the time when the Apostle penned this letter. But Christ was not only a high priest after the order of Melchisedek, but he was a high priest *forever*. Mark the language of the 22d verse: "By so much,"—that is, " by so much was Jesus made a surety of a better testament. And they truly were many priests, because they were not suffered to continue by reason of death: but this man, because he continueth forever, hath an unchangeable priesthood." While thus we have the apostle settling forever the truth that Christ is now and ever has been a priest after the order of Melchisedek, and never was a priest after any other order, let us look around once more.

My opponent, therefore, having rested the entire issue upon the fact that Christ was to be a high priest forever, after the order of Melchisedek, when he should be upon his throne, and the Apostle declaring that Christ is now a high priest forever, after the order of Melchisedek, we shall hereafter treat it as an established and admitted truth that the kingdom of Christ is now in existence, and not future.

In this fact is found the reason why Peter, in addressing the Church, called them "really priests." 1st Peter, 2d chapter and 9th verse, says, " But ye are a chosen generation—a royal priesthood." Royalty is something that belongs to the king's family alone. The same passage to which I have just referred, says, "Ye are a chosen generation, a royal priesthood, an holy nation, a peculiar people." Here we have four terms: nation, people, generation, and priesthood, all applied to what James and Paul called "Israel." If you will turn to the 10th chapter of Romans, and 19th verse, you will find a very vivid contrast to that which the Apostle affirms of that which he calls " the twelve tribes of Israel."

"But I say, Did not Israel know? First, Moses saith, I will provoke you to jealousy by them that are no people, and by a foolish nation I will anger you."

Let us pause and inquire what are the forms in which nations are formed to exist? There are three forms, and only that number, viz.: republics, oligarchies, and kingdoms. Of which one of these does the kingdom before us in its nature partake? Is it a kingdom, an oligarchy, or a republic? In republics all are equal, all are co-rulers. In oligarchies the few rule the many. A kingdom is the most simple of all the forms of government—the will of the king being the supreme law of the land.

I wish now to call your attention to several passages of scripture. Two of them—Romans, 10th chapter, 19th verse, and 1st Peter, 2d chapter and 9th verse—I have just read in your hearing. I call your attention to the language of Matthew, 17th chapter, 18th and 19th verses:

"And Jesus rebuked the devil, and he departed out of him: and the child was cured from that very hour. Then came the disciples to Jesus apart, and said, Why could not we cast him out?"

Also Acts, 15th chapter and 7th verse:

"And when there had been much disputing, Peter rose up and said unto them, Men and brethren, ye know how that a good while ago, God made choice among us, that the Gentiles, by my mouth, should hear the word of the gospel, and believe."

Romans, 14th chapter and 17th verse:

"For the kingdom of God is not meat and drink, but righteousness, and peace, and joy in the Holy Ghost."

The benefits of any kingdom are to be possessed and enjoyed only by the citizens of that kingdom. Mr. Stephenson has told us that he and his brethren are not in this kingdom, and if that be true, then the unavoidable conclusion is that they are not entitled to any of the rights and privileges of it. But let us inquire, what are the privileges and immunities of the kingdom of God? My opponent, and those who agree with him, may talk as much as they please about the peculiarities and privileges of other kingdoms. The kingdom before us, and its privileges and immunities, are widely different from other kingdoms —they are earthly and sensual, while the privileges and blessings of Christ's kingdom are righteousness, peace and joy in the Holy Spirit. Observe that the kingdom of which my opponent tells you, is an earthly, fleshly kingdom. He speaks of its running along from generation to generation, for a thousand years. Peter, in his first Epistle, 2d chapter and 5th verse, says:

"Ye also, as lively stones, are built up a spiritual house, a holy priesthood, to offer up spiritual sacrifices, acceptable to God by Jesus Christ."

In the kingdom of which Mr. Stephenson speaks, there will be male and female, just the same as now; but in the resurrection there will be neither male nor female—they neither marry nor are given in marriage,—but are as the angels of God in heaven. Such is the striking contrast between the kingdom of our Lord Jesus Christ, which is spiritual, and the kingdom of which my opponent speaks, which is earthly and sensual.

This kingdom being of a spiritual nature, its blessings will be spiritual. There are no such privileges connected with it as belong to the kingdoms of this earth. The privileges of a subject of an earthly kingdom, are to enjoy the result of his own toil and labor, and the protection and enjoyment of his domestic and other earthly privileges. But this kingdom of our Lord Jesus Christ is righteousness, peace and joy in the Holy Spirit. Observe the contrast between the Christian's hope and the hope spoken of by my opponent. The Christian hopes, not for an inheritance of acres of land, nor an abundant harvest of corn, nor for an abundant increase of flocks and herds. These all are destined to perish with the using; but on the contrary, the Apostle, in 1st Peter, 1st chapter, 3d and 5th verses, inclusive, says:

"Blessed be the God and Father of our Lord Jesus Christ, which, according to his abundant mercy, hath begotten us again unto a lively hope by the resurrection of Jesus Christ from the dead, to an inheritance incorruptible, and undefiled, and that fadeth not away, reserved in heaven for you, who are kept by the power of God through faith unto salvation, ready to be revealed in the last time."

The kingdom described by my opponent has its highest hope in perishable matters.

Let us now look around once more over the premises

before us. I now call your attention to one thrilling thought, penned by the Apostle Paul—Hebrews, 7th chapter and 19th verse—wherein he speaks of the bringing in of a "better hope":

"For the law made nothing perfect, but the bringing in of a better hope did; by the which we draw nigh unto God."

What can be the meaning of these words, "better hope"? I venture the assertion that these words point to something that never can take place on this globe.

Here I wish to pause and sum up the evidence as far as we have gone. We inquired, in the first place, as to the nature of the kingdom, and directed your minds to the truth that all governments are of one or another of three kinds, namely: republics, oligarchies, and monarchies. Which one of these is it that the kingdom of God shall belong to? Let us go to Colossians, 1st chapter and 13th verse, and there we find this language:

"Who hath delivered us from the power of darkness, and hath translated us into the kingdom of his dear Son:"

Let us look at both parts f this expression. Here is, in the first place, a striking contrast between the "power of darkness" and the "kingdom of God's dear Son." It is clear that every man is understood to be in one or in the other of these two. This is most rigidly true. If any man is not in the kingdom of God's dear Son, he is in the kingdom of the devil; and hence, as a matter of course, recognizing the devil as his master, to whom he shall stand or fall. But on the other hand, since the kingdom of Christ is set up on the earth, those who obey the truth pass out of the kingdom of darkness and out of the kingdom of the devil, into the kingdom of God's dear Son,—pass from under the authority of Satan to the authority of our Lord Jesus Christ. Every human being therefore upon earth, is in one or the other of these two conditions. If, therefore, my opponent and his friends are not now, at this very hour, in the kingdom of Christ, they are in the kingdom of the devil, and I will give them a hint that they had better make arrangements to emigrate from there as speedily as possible.

Let me just here bring in one other declaration. Go to Hebrews, 12th chapter and 28th verse: "Wherefore we receiving a kingdom which can not be moved, let us have grace, whereby we may serve God acceptably with reverence and godly fear." In Daniel, 2d chapter, 44th verse, we had the thought that the kingdom there spoken of was to be set up in the days of "these kings;" that is to say, in the days of the Roman Cæsars. Paul here says that he and his brethren are receiving it. He wrote that they were, even when he wrote receiving a kingdom that could not be removed. Having got out of the kingdom of the devil and into that of God's dear son, he says, let us now serve him with reverence and godly fear. Look at the word "into." How clearly and forcibly it fixes the thought that the apostle, when writing to the Hebrews, regarded himself as being within the kingdom of God's dear son. Now, either that kingdom was then in existence or it was not. If was not then in existence, then it was nothing. And if it was nothing, then Paul and all his brethren were already annihilated or reduced to nothing, for nothing larger than nothing can be put into nothing. I conclude, therefore, that the kingdom of God's dear son was not then nothing, but that it was in exist ence when Paul wrote.

One thought more just here. Go to Revelations, 1st chapter. We have already brought before you this expression, but I will bring it before your minds once more. Read the 9th verse: "I, John, who also am your brother, and companion in tribulation, and in the kingdom and patience of Jesus Christ, was in the isle that is called Patmos, for the word of God, and for the testimony of Jesus Christ." Here we have a confirmation of the truth that the apostle was then in the kingdom, if John wrote the truth. Now, he either wrote the truth or did not. If he wrote the truth, then it is clear that the kingdom was in existence in his day.

We have found, in the course of this examination, three

things: first, that Jesus Christ is now a priest af the order of Mechisedek; second, that he is now on his throne (for it was admitted by my opponent that Christ was to be a priest after the order of Melchisedek when he should be on his throne;) and, lastly, we have just now found that the kingdom of God was in actual existence when Paul wrote. For if this be not taken to be true, we have the extraordinary alternative that Paul and all his brethren were nothing, and, therefore, we have one vast heap of nothing "translated" into nothing; and if that argument does not amount to absolutely nothing but a huge pile of nonsense, then I am not a competent judge of the matter. All this must be so, or, on the other hand, the kingdom of God's dear son was in existence when Paul wrote that he and his brethren had been translated into it. And if it was in existence at that time, it shall never be overthrown, and, therefore, shall stand forever. Therefore, if those who have escaped from the power of darkness and been translated into this kingdom shall continue loyal to it, they have no reason to fear, for the power of the king is pledged to carry them safely and triumphantly though.

---

## NEG.—J. M. STEPHENSON.—SEVENTH SPEECH.

I wish to notice a few things in the speeches of my opponent having reference, or at least, as I suppose, designed to have reference to the positions I have answered in the progress of this discussion. My opponent said that Christ was now a high priest after the order of Melchisedek, and, therefore, that he is now upon his throne. The Apostle Paul, in the 5th chapter of Hebrews, and at the 5th and 6th verses, quotes the language of the great God: "So, also, Christ glorified not himself, to be made an high priest; but he that said unto him, Thou art my son, to-day have I begotten thee. As he saith also in another place, Thou art a priest forever, after the order of Melchisedek."

Now, I can demonstrate, upon precisely the same principle of reasoning, that at the time David wrote the 110th Psalm, Christ was upon his throne, for David says in that psalm: "The Lord *hath* sworn, and will not repent; Thou ART a priest forever, after the order of Melchisedek." Take, now, the 15th, 16th and 17th verses of the 7th chapter of Hebrews: "And it is yet far more evident, for that after the similitude of Melchisedek there ariseth another priest, who is made, not after the law of a carnal commandment, but after the power of an endless life. For he testifieth, Thou art a priest forever, after the order of Melchisedek." Now, it is apparent at a single glance that if the tense of the verb used in the epistle to the Hebrews shows that when Paul wrote Christ was a priest after the order of Melchisedek, then the tense of the verb used in the 110th Psalm shows that he was a priest after the order of Melchisedeck when David wrote this psalm.

I wish to call your attention, here, to the fact that the words "nation" and "tribes" are used synonymously. So, also, with regard to the word "family." "Families," "nations" and "tribes" are used interchangeably, and one may be substituted for the other without violating the sense. In one place in Genesis it is said that in Abraham and in his seed should all the "families" of the earth be blessed; and in another place it is said that in his seed all the "nations" of the earth should be blessed. These words are exchanged in a great number of instances for the simple purpose of avoiding tautology.

Your attention was called to the statement of the apostle that the kingdom was not meat and drink, but righteousness, peace and joy in the Holy Ghost. Now, our friends of the Disciple Church say they are *in* the kingdom. I wonder whether they do without MEAT and DRINK. If eating and drinking are incompatible with the condition of being in the kingdom, I can not see but the objection lies as much against them as it does against us. If meat and drink are not compatible with the reign of Christ, then my Campbellite friends can not be in Christ's kingdom. I am willing to compare his church with ours and see which of the two is the most fleshy in its manifestations. I stand ready to measure swords with him upon that question whenever and wherever he sees fit.

Again my opponent says, that he objects to our view of the nature of Christ's kingdom, because it contemplates a succession of natural generations, and that he regards as inconsistent with the Kingdom of God. But let me ask him, are not he and his brethren, according to his own assertions, now in that kingdom, and yet have they no such thing as natural generations in the Campbellite Church? If they have natural generations in their kingdom, why should they urge the very same thing against us? Now, all I have to say about this matter, is this: that if in the Kingdom of God there shall ever be found more fleshliness, and covetousness, and love of houses and lands, than there is in the Disciple Church to-day, then God Almighty deliver me from that kingdom. What do they do? Do they not add farm to farm and field to field? Do they not treasure up hoards of silver and gold as well as any body else? If they do not buy up all the land there is around where they live, it is not their fault—it is only because they have not the means to do it with. I deny that there is any evidence whatever, that the church to which Mr. Russell belongs has any less worldly mindedness in it than ours, notwithstanding the fact that they profess to be even now in the Kingdom of God, which is not meat and drink, but righteousness, peace and joy in the Holy Spirit.

I will tell him what some of the characteristics of the coming age will be. It will be an age in which there will be none of these great land monopolies that now curse the earth and exclude God's poor from the use of the soil. It will be an age of free soil, where the rich shall no longer oppress the poor.

I would say just here, and it is a fact that should not be lost sight of, that the antithesis of the word "spiritual" is not "literal," but it is simply "animal." Now, if a church composed of flesh and blood can be "spiritual," why cannot a kingdom that is "spiritual" be likewise composed of flesh and blood? "Men who live in glass houses ought to be very careful how they throw stones."

But my opponent says his hope and that of his brethren is in Heaven, while ours is on the earth. Well, I would rather have a hope on earth, or in Heaven either, than to have none at all, and that is really the condition they are in so far as the kingdom is concerned, because, according to their own statements, they have already got the kingdom and have none to hope for in the future. Our hope is for the coming of our Lord Jesus Christ. The title to our kingdom is vested in him. When he comes we shall possess with him the kingdom, and if he never comes we shall never get it. When he comes he will set up his throne in accordance with prophecy, and then shall our hope be realized. The apostle John, in the 22d chapter of Revelations, says, "Behold I come quickly, and my reward is with me, to give every man according to his work." Our reward is with him, and our hope is that when he shall come he will invite the blessed of his Father to come and inherit the kingdom. He will share the inheritance with all the saints of the Most High.

I shall now resume the affirmative part of the discussion where I left it off. I was showing you the inconsistency of the position that the church is the kingdom. I was showing that so far from the church being the kingdom, the church was promised the kingdom as a reward for fealty. Christ said it was hard for a rich man to enter into the Kingdom of God—as hard as it was for a camel to go through the eye of a needle. My friend, Mr. Russell, is it as hard for a rich man to get into your kingdom as it is for a camel to go through the eye of a needle? Will not your church turn out half a dozen poor men where they will not turn out one rich man for the very same offense? Even your ministers will bow low to a rich man. And yet how different from this is the Kingdom of God! The road is so narrow, the gate is so straight, that a rich man cannot get into it with his riches at all. That description will not apply to your kingdom at all. What right, then, have you to claim that your church is the Kingdom of God? I like consistency, even in error.

Again, Christ said, "Suffer little children to come unto me, and forbid them not, for of such is the Kingdom of Heaven." Has my opponent become all of a sudden converted into a Pedo-Baptist? In his church-kingdom little children have no part. Did you turn the children all out on the day of Pentecost? You must either take the position that Christ on the day of Pentecost excommunicated all these little children, or that they remained within the kingdom and are in it still. And here again I say, "Consistency, thou art a jewel." What did Christ mean when he said, "Suffer little children to come unto me, for of such is the kingdom of Heaven?" It is easily understood when you admit the true nature of the kingdom. When Israel shall be brought back into their own land, the two branches re-united into one kingdom, and when they shall dwell in the land, they shall be greatly multiplied—so says the inspired prophet of God, Ezekiel—and thus will there be children in the Kingdom of Jesus Christ. Admit the true nature of the Kingdom of God, and all difficulty disappears, like fog before the morning sun.

Let us go a step further. Christ, who shall come, and shall sit upon the throne of his glory, invites the church to come and inherit—what? To come and inherit *the Church?* The absurdity of the thing speaks for itself. It is not that. He invites them to come and inherit the "Kingdom," prepared for them from the foundation of the world. Whatever that kingdom shall be, it is plain that it is not to be established *until* the time when Christ shall set upon the throne of his glory, and all nations shall stand before him; for it is then, and not till then, that he invites his people to come and inherit the kingdom. Can we imagine that Christ will use this language after the "blessed of the Father" have already inherited, possessed and enjoyed that kingdom for eighteen hundred years and more? They have already been that long in full possession of the kingdom, if my opponent's position is true, that the church is that kingdom.

Again, Christ told his disciples that he would not drink of the juice of the grape again until he dank it anew in his Father's—church? No; in his Father's *Kingdom*. The disciples asked Christ, "Wilt thou at this time restore again the *kingdom* to Israel?" They did not ask him if he would restore the church to Israel. Now, a thing cannot be restored until it has first had an existence, and afterwards has been overthrown or destroyed; then it can be restored. Now, if the kingdom meant the church, there is an insuperable difficulty in the way; for the church had not been overthrown or destroyed, and therefore to talk of restoring the church would have been sheer nonsense. But apply the language to the kingdom of Israel, and let it refer to a restoration of that nation at a time future, and there is not a particle of difficulty, but all is clear and simple.

Turn with me now to Hebrews, 12th chapter and 28th verse:

"Wherefore we receiving a kingdom which cannot be moved, let us have grace, whereby we may serve God acceptably with reverence and godly fear."

The kingdom that is here spoken of as being received by the apostle and his brethren is represented as being a kingdom which cannot be moved—a kingdom that shall remain forever—and from this very fact we learn that other kingdoms are to be removed out of the way. The time is near at hand when all the nations of the earth shall come up to Mt. Zion to Christ the Judge of all the earth and the King of kings—the Mediator of the new covenant—and he shall administer justice and judgment unto them. Did they then in fact come up to Mt. Zion on the day of Pentecost? Was Jesus Christ in person there on that day? Did they come on that day to "the spirits of just men made perfect," or to the "general assembly and church of the first born?" Did they come in fact on that day, or did they only then come by faith? They did not come in fact we know. They came by faith. And why may not the kingdom have come by faith also? But we believe that from the standpoint marked down by the apostle, the people of God, whether living or dead, having been raised from the slumbers of the grave, shall receive a kingdom that cannot be moved.

Paul tells the church in another place: "It is through much tribulation that we enter the kingdom." Is there much tribulation to pass through in order to get into the church of my opponent? I could go into their church in the town of Buchanan, in Iowa, and everywhere, by endorsing their creed. On these conditions, any rich man can go right into their church without the least particle of tribulation. It is not through much tribulation that we enter the church, but it is through much tribulation we are to enter into the kingdom of God.

Turn, if you please, to the Epistle of James, 2d chapter and 5th verse:

"Hearken, my beloved brethren, Hath not God chosen the poor of this world rich in faith, and heirs of the kingdom which he hath promised to them that love him?"

He speaks here of the poor of this world being heirs—heirs of what? Heirs of the *church?* The poor do not certainly inherit the church—they are not the heirs of the church. We are told by the apostle that they are "heirs of the kingdom." Mark, the passage makes these Christians heirs (not possessors,) of a future kingdom, thirty years after the day of Pentecost. But if the church is the kingdom, they were then possessors of an existing kingdom.

Peter says: "Add to your faith virtue, and to virtue knowledge, and to knowledge temperance, and to temperance patience," and so on, godliness, brotherly kindness and charity. For if we do so, what shall we have? "An abundant entrance into the everlasting kingdom of our Lord and Savior Jesus Christ." How would it read to substitute for the everlasting kingdom in this promise the church? How would it sound to tell them that if they possessed such and such noble christian graces, an abundant entrance should be administered unto them into the everlasting church? But apply this to a future kingdom, and it will all be plain. There is a peculiar and special difficulty just here, in view of the meaning and rise of the original Greek word here translated kingdom, (*Basilei*,) if it is translated "church." That Greek term has in it essentially the idea of royalty. Basileus signifies a royal sovereign—and basilei a kingdom reigned over by a sovereign. Ecclesia, the term for church, is never translated "kingdom"—nor is there any more propriety in translating basilei by the word church, than there would be in translating ecclesia by the word kingdom. The word basilei cannot be translated church without the greatest absurdity in a great variety of instances. We are told that they "shall come from the East and the West, the North and the South, and shall sit down with Abraham, Isaac and Jacob in"—in what? In the church? The sentence would be ridiculous.

I now propose, if I have time, to look at some of the objections of my opponent. Let us inquire a little in regard to Christ's coming in the clouds of heaven at the time of his second advent. The shining ones said to the apostles: "Ye men of Gallilee why stand ye here gazing up into heaven—this same Jesus shall return again in like manner as ye have seen him go into heaven." How did he go into heaven? He arose and went from them and a bright cloud received him out of their sight.

In the 30th verse of the 24th chapter of Matthew, he is represented as coming "in the clouds of heaven with power and great glory." In Revelations 1st chapter and 7th verse, it is written, "Behold he cometh with clouds and every eye shall see him and they also which pierced him and all the kindreds of the earth shall wail because of him." Will my opponent insist upon wresting the 13th verse of the 7th chapter of Daniel from its connections so as to make the son go to the Father instead of coming down to this earth in the clouds of heaven? John says, he *came*, Daniel uses the word "come." What does that word mean? Surely it means to approximate to the person speaking. We know that very well. In regard to the personage or personages intended by the words ancient of days, it evidently does not refer to the Father of our Lord. An excellent Hebrew scholar says, the original word might with perfect propriety be rendered in the plural—"ancients." It doubtless refers to the angels of God who shall attend Christ when he comes to judge the world.

## AFF.—P. T. RUSSELL.—EIGHTH SPEECH.

I shall commence as nearly as possible at the point where we closed. On Saturday last the issue was formed between me and my opponent as to the great city which is to be the capital of the new earth. Into that city all the righteous are to enter, by my friend's admission. The nations are to bring their glory and honor into it and those outside are denomined dogs and sorcerers and so on. Those on the inside, as he said on Saturday, will all be kings and emperors. Let me ask over whom will they rule? If all the wicked are outside of this city, and forever to stay out, and all the righteous inside, and forever to stay in, how are all these kings and emperors to rule over them that are outside of the city walls. A wall fifteen hundred miles high cuts them off from their subjects, I do not see how he can say that all of those who are within those walls are kings and emperors unless they take turns in ruling, and whenever it comes to that I think they would not be a great while in getting up a quarrel about who should rule first. Here then is the first difficulty that grows out of my friend's view of this great city—the royal personages inside cannot rule over any beings in the universe from their isolated position unless they rule over each other by turns. There is a wall fifteen hundred miles high between them and their proper subjects—the "dogs and sorcerers" cannot get in and the "kings and emperors" cannot get out.

I wish now to present to your minds another contrast. Turn to the 3d chapter of Matthew and 2d verse, John the Baptist proclaimed in the wilderness of Judea, "Repent ye, for the kingdom of heaven is at hand." In Luke 10th chapter and 11th verse, Christ also tells his disciples, "Be ye sure of this — that the kingdom of God is come nigh unto you." Here the kingdom of God is said to be "at hand," and it is said to have come nigh. Mark the beginning of the 2d chapter of 2d Thessalonians.

"Now we beseech you brethren, by the coming of our Lord Jesus Christ, and by our gathering together unto him, That ye be not soon shaken in mind, or be troubled neither by spirit, nor by word, nor by letter as from us, that the day of Christ is at hand."

Let no man deceive you by any means. The amount of this instruction given by Christ to his apostles is just this. If any one says to you that the day of the Lord is as near at hand as his kingdom do not believe one word of it. While John the Baptist, the Savior himself, the twelve and the seventy, said the kingdom of heaven was at hand. Paul writing more than thirty years afterwards says to his brethren, if any one tells you that the day of the Lord is at hand he is a liar and the truth is not in him. How can this be if both are to come at one and the same time? If this kingdom of God is to be set up according to Mr. Stephenson, when the Lord comes hereafter, then it is clear that when Paul wrote that the kingdom was not at hand, he stands convicted of having written a falsehood. He says in the same chapter from which I have just quoted, and immediately following the preceding quotation. "For that day shall not come except there come a falling away first, and that man of sin be revealed, the son of perdition," and so on. I repeat it once more that the "kingdom of God" and the "day of the Lord" were one of them, just as near as the other at the time Paul wrote if they came at the same time. Either Paul was a false teacher, or else every one who teaches that they were to come at one and the same time is a false teacher.

Judge ye, for yourselves, on whom you will rely. One of the two was at hand when John spoke — the other was not at hand when Paul wrote. Of one the Savior said it had come nigh; of the other Paul said it was a long way off. In Matthew 25th chapter, and 19th verse, we are told that "after a long time the lord of those servants cometh and reckoneth with them." Here then we find an irreconcilable contrast between the kingdom of God and the time spoken of as "the day of the Lord."

Let us now turn our attention to other matters which we desire to bring before you. My opponent has located the second coming of Christ more than a thousand years before the final resurrection and judgment; and yet, in his very last speech, he told you that every eye should see him and all the nations of the earth should wail because of him. When he made the last statement he told you the truth, but when he said the Savior would appear a thousand years before the last resurrection, he told you what cannot be true. He is here directly in conflict with himself.

How does the word of God dispose of this matter? says the Savior—in Matthew 25th chapter, 31st and 32d verse.

"When the Son of Man shall come in his glory, and all the holy angels with him, then shall he sit upon the throne of his glory: And before him shall be gathered all nations; and he shall separate them one from another, as a shepherd divideth his sheep from the goats."

When is it that all nations are to be gathered together before him? Answer. When he comes. It is said in the 24th chapter of Matthew, and 30th verse, and also in Revelations 1st chapter and 7th verse, that he shall come with clouds and with power and great glory, and that every eye shall see him, and they also that pierced him and that all kindreds of the earth shall wail because of him.

It is clear from the manner in which the two are conjoined in the language just referred to, that the time of the coming of Christ is coincident with the time of the final judgment and resurrection. It is at that very time, (as Paul declares 2 Corinthians, 5th chapter and 10th verse,) that you and I must appear before the judgment seat of Christ, to give an account for the deeds done in the body, and then we too shall hear the final sentence of the Judge Eternal concerning us. And when this is done (1 Corinthians, 15th chapter,) the Son gives up the kingdom to God the Father, "that God may be all in all." The time of his coming being the time of the last resurrection, then all ruling power will be taken from Death, and then will occur what is related in the 110th Psalm: "The Lord said unto my Lord, Sit thou at my right hand till I make thy foes thy footstool." Paul, the apostle, in the 15th chapter of 1 Corinthians, has quoted and commented upon this very passage, and he there declares that the Savior is to remain at God's right hand until his enemies are all subdued, and one of those enemies, and the last that shall be subdued, is Death. Death will not be subdued until all ruling power is taken from him—all ruling power will not be taken from death until the last human being has been brought out from under Death's dominion. Consequently Christ must sit where he now is upon the right hand of the Father until the resurrection of the last member of the human family. Then, Death being destroyed, his power demolished, the Son gives up his position at the right hand of the Father, gives up the kingdom to God, even the Father, that God may be all in all.

I have already anticipated, that while my opponent places the coming of Christ at the beginning of his reign. Paul, on the other hand, places it at its consummation, when he gives up the kingdom to the Father. Mr. Stephenson represented the Savior as going to Heaven, remaining there for century upon century, and then coming back to this earth to prepare a kingdom for those who are to be kings and to reign in his temporal kingdom. Hear John, 14th chapter, 2d and 3d verses:

"In my Father's house are many mansions: if it were not so, I would have told you. I go to prepare a place for you. And if I go and prepare a place for you, I will come again, and receive you unto myself; that where I am, there ye may be also."

Does the Savior say, "I will come and stay here?" No.

He says, "I will come and receive you to myself, that where I am there ye may be also."

Let us now pass to look at some other interesting matters. My friend has claimed that there is to be a probation of a thousand years after the coming of Christ. If Christ is to judge the quick and dead at his second coming, at his appearing and kingdom, then as a natural consequence there can not be a thousand years of probation to transpire after his coming, and before the final judgment. The time *of his appearing and kingdom* is the time of his giving up the kingdom to the Father. Go to Matthew, 24th chapter, 37th to 39th verse, inclusive:

"But as the days of Noe were, so shall also the coming of the Son of man be. For as in the days that were before the flood, they were eating and drinking, marrying and giving in marriage, until the day that Noe entered into the ark, and knew not until the flood came, and took them all away: so shall also the coming of the Son of man be."

When the flood came, not a solitary human being but those who had before obeyed the Lord, escaped. Not one solitary moment was given them for preparation. Now, the Savior says the coming of the Son of man shall be just as was the coming of the flood; and as not one solitary rebel then escaped, neither shall one solitary rebel escape when the Son of man shall come. The rebel shall receive the reward of a rebel, and an obedient servant shall receive the reward of the obedient. But to make "assurance doubly sure," go with me now, and let us see what we have it. 2d Thessalonians, 1st chapter and 7th verse:

"And to you who are troubled, rest with us, when the Lord Jesus shall be revealed from heaven with his mighty angels."

They are to be driven away when he comes—not a thousand years afterward.

Having this matter set thus clearly before us, let us look once more at this remarkable expression: "Shall be punished with everlasting destruction from the presence of the Lord, and from the glory of his power, when he shall come to be admired in all them that believe." There are but two great events that are called in the Holy Scriptures "the coming of the Lord." The first is where he came as "a man of sorrows, and acquainted with grief;" the second will be when he shall come again "without a sin, offering unto salvation." And at this very time, when he shall come to be glorified in all his saints, then, at that very time, is he to punish all his foes, and drive them from the presence of the Lord forever, and from the glory of his power.

Now if Paul tells the truth, where is your thousand years of probation! I have heard of a certain thing said to be harder to do than for a camel to go through the eye of a needle; but it would be a great deal easier for a thousand camels to go through the eye of the finest cambric needle, than it will be for my opponent to get himself out of this difficulty.

Let us now turn and look at one other little matter. And here again we have presented to us the spectacle of Stephenson against Stephenson. The good Book tells us that a kingdom divided against itself cannot stand. Let us see how long Mr. Stephenson's theory is likely to stand when divided, as it now is, against itself. He has spoken of "heirship" and "possession" as being synonymous. He declared that a man could not be heir to anything and possess it at the same time; and this declaration he made in the very next breath after saying that heirship and possession were synonymous terms. Are there any ladies or gentlemen here who have inherited real estate from their parents? You are just as much an heir of your ancestor now as you were before you entered into full possession of the property. I want my friend to bear in mind hereafter, that a man may be both heir and possessor at one and the same time. Let us try to speak of these things as they are, and not as our fancies would have them. We are told that the words "nation" and "family" are synonymous. I receive that in a qualified manner. Go to Ephesians, 3d chapter and 15th verse:

"Of whom the whole family in heaven and earth is named."

This is the Lord's family he is speaking of. Now if you had no son nor daughter, nor any member of your family, in Oregon, for instance, could I, with any degree of propriety, in speaking of you, use the term, "the whole family in Oregon and Indiana?" Certainly not. But on the other hand, if you had children in Indiana, and in Oregon also, I could use such an expression with perfect propriety. Just so the Apostle, speaking of the members of the Savior's family, said, "Of whom the whole family in heaven and on earth is named." And here, too, is the reason why the Savior said "All power is given unto me in heaven and on earth." The earth is only one province of the Savior's kingdom—the other is above us.

I will merely pause for one moment, just here, to inquire: Will my opponent affirm that a "kingdom" is not a "nation?" If he will say that a nation can not be a kingdom, nor a kingdom a nation, I will acknowledge that there is some little consistency in what he says; but until he does so all his talk is vain.

Let us turn, once more, to the coming of Christ to the "Ancient of days." He suggests that we take the words "of days" out of the sentence and it will be very plain and easily to be understood according to his interpretation of the passage. Well, I do not know what we might make out of the Word of God in many passages by taking out a word here and a word there, if we were inclined to do so. I will adopt his suggestion and I will make a curiosity. I have just as good a right to take out any other word I please from any sentence found in the Bible as he has to take the word "days" out of the passage in question. Let us see: "Let him that stole, steal." There is a very unwarrantable perversion of an idea, for the true reading of the sentence is: "Let him that stole, steal *no more.*" I have just as good a right to take any word I please out of a sentence of Holy Writ as my opponent has.

## NEG.—J. M. STEPHENSON—EIGHTH SPEECH.

I stated, upon the authority of one of the best Hebrew scholars in the United States, that the word "days" might be left out of the expression "ancient of days" used in the English version of the Bible. We find in the 2d chapter of Colossians the language: "Let no man, therefore, judge you in meat, or in drink, or in respect of a holy day, or of the new moon, or of the sabbath days, which are a shadow of things to come; but the body is of Christ." Many translators leave out the word "days" in this passage, leaving the word "sabbaths." And so in many other instances. The Bible is full of them. The Hebrew word elohim has singular verbs and pronouns representing it. So of the Hebrew pronoun rendered "ancient of days."

My opponent wants to know if all the righteous are to reign and to be kings, over whom they are to reign. They will reign over the nations of the earth, as has been already demonstrated a number of times during the progress of this debate. By reference to the 4th chapter of Micah and the 2d chapter of Isaiah you will find that at the time when the word of the Lord shall go forth from Zion, the nations will still be in a mortal state, and all nations shall come up to Jerusalem, saying: "Come, let us go up to the mountain of the Lord, and to the house of the God of Jacob; and he will teach us of his ways, and we will walk in his paths." You will find, by referring to Revelations, 20th chapter and 3d verse, that an angel puts a seal upon the old dragon after he has been cast into the bottomless pit, that he should deceive the nations no more till the thousand years should be finished. Now, if the nations should not then be in a state that rendered them susceptible of being deceived, where is the necessity that God should thus chain the adversary and cast him into the pit and put a seal on him to keep him from deceiving them any more UNTIL the thousand years should be fulfilled? It would be like chaining the wolf after he had killed off the last sheep of the flock, if the nations had all been destroyed before the dragon had been chained. The nations, to prevent the deceiving of which Satan is chained, will be the subjects over whom Christ and the saints shall reign. Hence it is said that they reigned with Christ a thousand years. While, as has been shown, Christ and his saints are within the city—while the throne of the Lamb is in the city, and the saints reign with him — without are nations, and these nations diseased, and within the city is medicine to heal their maladies. They must, therefore, be mortal, and upon probation, or they would not need healing. That these nations are upon the earth is evident from the 24th verse of the 21st chapter, which reads: "And the nations of them which are saved shall walk in the light of it; and the kings of the earth do bring their glory and honor into (to) it." These mortal nations will be the subjects in the kingdom. In the 2d chapter and 26th verse, Christ says: "And he that overcometh, and keepeth my works unto the end, to him will I give power over the nations." The saints will be the rulers and these nations the subjects. While the kingdom and dominion of the whole earth shall be given to Christ and all the saints of the Most High, as a first party, there will be all nations as a second party to serve and obey. See Daniel vii: 13, 14, 27. Now, these nations come to the city of Jerusaem—the city of the great king. My opponent says they can not get in. Very well. The original word, rendered IN, is as often translated BY and TO as it is translated INTO; and if they come to the city it is quite sufficient for our purpose. We will not stop to quibble about that. The nations come to the city, bringing their glory and honor to it. It does not follow that they go into the city at all. These nations are without, while the saints of God and the Lamb are within; and within the walls of that city is also the tree of life, and "the leaves of the tree are for the healing of the nations." The obedient go through the gates into the city, but the disobedient stay outside.

But my friend Mr. Russell says that the time of Christ's coming and the final resurrection are one and the same, and, therfore, there can be no period of a thousand years probation. Go with me, if you please, to the 20th chapter of Revelations and 4th and 5th verses, and you will read the following language: "And I saw thrones, and they sat upon them, and judgment was given unto them; and I saw the souls of them that were beheaded for the witness of Jesus, and for the word of God, and which had not worshipped the beast, neither his image, neither had received his mark upon their foreheads, or in their hands; and they lived and reigned with Christ a thousand years. But the rest of the dead lived not again until the thousand years were finished. This is the first resurrection." In the 4th verse we have the copulative conjunction *and*, but in the 5th verse the disjunctive conjunction *but* is used, showing the contrast between those first mentioned and those that follow. "And they lived and reigned with Christ a thousand years. But the rest of the dead lived not *again until* the thousand years were finished." Thus teaching that one thousand years shall intervene between the two resurrections. At the 6th verse we find a record of the first resurrection: "Blessed and holy is he that hath part in the first resurrection. On such the second death hath no power, but they shall be priests of God and of Christ, and shall reign with him a thousand years." At the 12th verse we find a record of the second resurrection at the end of the thousand years: "And I saw the dead, small and great, (high and low degree,) stand before God; and the books were opened, and another book was opened, which is the book of life, and the dead were judged out of those things which were written in the books, according to their works."

But let us see how it is about this wall of which my opponent speaks, that is fifteen hundred miles high, so that the nations outside can not get in and the saints who are inside can not get out. He concludes, from his statement, that, as a necessary consequence, the saints, if they rule at all, must rule over one another within the walls of the city. Let us, in the first place, look at my friend's mathematics. He stated that the city was fifteen hundred miles square. John does not say so. If you have a field that has just one hundred rods in its measure, and that field should be square, there would be just twenty-five rods on each of the four sides. The city was measured fifteen hundred miles, and it was square. That would give just three hundred and seventy-five miles on each side. The length and the breadth and the hight of the city are equal. But you know there is always a certain symmetry and proportion to be observed in the length and width and hight of a house. The very sense of the term rendered *equal*, signifies proportion. The city is to be of fair and beautiful proportions. This is what is meant by the revelator. And there is to be no night there. The gates of the city will not be closed at night, for there will be no night there. My opponent never seems to look at a text to see what it means.

But he has learned another strange thing—he has discovered that the word "all," in one place means all, while in another place it signifies only one third. He has found out that I have changed my position—that I have taken the position that the wicked dead at the time of Christ's coming will not be raised until the end of a thousand years. And secondly that the very men who actually pierced Christ will be raised from the dead when Christ comes in order to look upon him. I will answer this right here. If he will answer the question as to whether the three thousand souls that were present on the day of Pentecost, personally killed Jesus Christ as Peter charged them with having done, then I will answer his question as to those who "shall look upon him whom they pierced. Before the assembled multitude at Jerusalem gathered together out of seventeen different nations, Peter said, "Ye have killed the Prince of Life." Had the persons he was addressing actually crucified the Prince of Life? No. Their nation however had done it, and they were held responsible for it. Upon the same principle the last living generation of the Jews who shall dwell in Palestine at the time of Christ's second advent shall "look upon him whom they have pierced." Christ declared that all the blood shed by his holy prophets from the blood of righteous Abel to the blood of Zachariah who was slain between the porch and the altar, was shed by those whom he was then addressing. They had not done it personally, we know that very well, but they belonged to the same race of those who had done it. That the language: "They shall look on him whom they pierced," refers to the generation of the Jewish people that shall be living in the land of Palestine, whither they shall have been gathered together out of all nations upon the earth, at the time of Christ's second coming, is evident from Zechariah 12th chapter and 7th and 8th verses, where the prophet says:

"The Lord also shall save the tents of Judah first, that the glory of the house of David and the glory of the inhabitants of Jerusalem do not magnify themselves against Judah. In that day shall the Lord defend the inhabitants of Jerusalem; and he that is feeble among them at that day shall be as David; and the house of David shall be as God, as the angel of the Lord before them."

Here we see clearly that those who are to look on him whom they have pierced are the Jews, who after being scattered abroad among all nations that dwell on the face of the earth, are afterward restored to the tents of Judah in the land of Palestine.

In another place the Lord declares by the mouth of the prophet that "I will gather all nations together against Jerusalem and there will I plead for my people." At the end of the period of their dispersion, the Jews will be gathered back into their own land, and then all nations will be gathered together in hostile array against them. The great conflict between Christ and the assembled nations is recorded in Rev. xix: 11-16: "And I saw heaven opened, and behold a white horse; and he that sat upon him was called Faithful and True, and in righteousness he doth judge and make war. His eyes were as a flame of fire, and on his head were many crowns; and he had a name written that no man knew but he himself. And he was clothed with a vesture dipped in blood; and his name is called The Word of God. And the armies which were in heaven followed him upon white horses, clothed in fine linen, white and clean. And out of his mouth goeth a sharp sword, that with it he should smite the nations; and he shall rule them with a rod of iron; and he treadeth the winepress of the fierceness and wrath of Almighty God. And he hath on his vesture and on his thigh a name written, KING OF KINGS, AND LORD OF LORDS." Zech. xiv: 1-5: "Behold, the day of the Lord cometh, and thy spoil shall be divided into the midst of thee. For I will gather all nations against Jerusalem to battle; and the city shall be taken, and the houses rifled, and the women ravished; and half of the city shall go forth into captivity and the residue of the people shall not be cut off from the city. Then shall the Lord go forth, and fight against those nations, as when he fought in the day of battle. And his feet shall stand in that day upon the Mount of Olives, which is before Jerusalem on the east, and the Mount of Olives shall cleave in the midst thereof toward the east and toward the west, and there shall be a very great valley; and half the mountain shall remove toward the north, and half of it toward the south. And ye shall flee to the valley of the mountains; for the valley of the mountains shall reach unto Azal; yea, ye shall flee, like as ye fled from before the earthquake in the days of Uzziah king of Judah; and the Lord my God shall come, and all the saints with thee." Joel iii: 1, 2: "For, behold, in those days, and in that time, when I shall bring again the captivity of Judah and Jerusalem, I will also gather all nations, and will bring them down into the valley of Jehoshaphat, and will plead with them there for my people, and for my heritage Israel, whom they have scattered among the nations, and parted my land."

The world will be represented in the last great battle. When Christ comes to overthrow the assembled nations, every eye shall see him, and they that pierced him, the Jews in that land.

## AFF.—P. T. RUSSELL—NINTH SPEECH.

Third Day, Tuesday, October 2d, 10 A. M.

The morning of the last day of this protracted discussion has arrived. It will be our purpose on this day as far as possible to sum up the evidence that has been adduced and submit the same to the arbitrament of your judgments. But while this shall be our purpose there are some things that require at our hands a somewhat critical notice. And first I wish to call your attention to this fact, that there is no where in the holy scriptures a solitary place, where the Lord has promised to restore Israel a *third time*. Where he has promised to deliver them a *third time* from bondage. And while I call your attention first to this fact we shall find the record of God's promise to restore them a *second* time, in Isaiah 11th chapter, and 11th and 16th verses inclusive, in the following language:

"And it shall come to pass in that day, that the Lord shall set his hand again the second time to recover the remnant of his people, which shall be left, from Assyria, and from Egypt, and from Pathros, and from Cush, and from Elam, and from Shinar, and from Hamath, and from the islands of the sea. And he shall set up an ensign for the nations, and shall assemble the outcasts of Israel, and gather together the dispersed of Judah from the four corners of the earth. The envy also of Ephraim shall depart, and the adversaries of Judah shall be cut off. Ephraim shall not envy Judah, and Judah shall not vex Ephraim. But they shall fly upon the shoulders of the Philistines toward the west; they shall spoil them of the east together; they shall lay their hand upon Edom and Moab; and the children of Ammon shall obey them. And the Lord shall utterly destroy the tongue of the Egyptain sea; and with his mighty wind shall he shake his hand over the river, and shall smite it in the seven streams, and make men go over dryshod. And there shall be a highway for the remnant of his people, which shall be left, from Assyria; like as it was to Israel in the day that he came up out of the land of Egypt."

Mark verse 11th—"And it shall come to pass in that day that the Lord shall set his hand again the *second time* to recover the remnant of his people which shall be left." Did he set his hand the first time to recover them from Egypt? Did he recover them from Egypt, and was not that the first time? And while I ask this question, you who are familiar with the bible know it is true—that it must be answered in the affirmative. Here, then, is the first time that the Lord "set his hand" to bring Israel up. The second time was when he "set his hand" to bring them up from the Babylonian captivity, and as there is nowhere within the lids of the Bible a voluntary promise to bring them up a third time, there is no evidence whatever in the Bible to show that God will ever restore, or that he has ever promised to restore, or to "bring them up" from their present dispersed condition. Again I ask you to mark the language contained in verse 11—"The Lord shall set his hand again the *second time* to recover the remnant of his people which shall be left." From where? Answer—" From Assyria," one place; " From Egypt," two places; " From Pathros," three places, and "from Cush." Here let us pause one moment. If he is going to call up his people from a country called " Cush," must it not be while there is such a country in existence? Of course it must be so. But long in the past has that people passed away from the face of the earth. The dark wave of oblivion has rolled over them for hundreds of years, and on earth as a people, they are known now no more. And thus we have cumulative evidence of the fact that the deliverance referred to in the passage before us, was a deliverance that is past and not future. But let us return to the passage we were reading. It is also said in the same verse, that he shall bring them "from Elam, and from Shinar, and from Hamath." Here are three other peoples or nations named, out of which the remnant of his people should be brought up, and no one of those three nations now exists upon the face of the globe. This second setting of his hand to recover them must be in the past and not in the future. At the time of the restoration of the Jews from the Babylonish captivity, there was a nation called "Cush," and all those other peoples and nations then existed, and by bringing up the Jews from those nations, and restoring them to their own land, the promise of the Lord was then fulfilled.

Examine, if you please, the last verse of the same chapter:

"And there shall be a highway for the remnant of his people, which shall be left, from Assyria; like as it was to Israel in the day that he came up out of the land of Egypt."

Of what time is the prophet here speaking? What restoration is prefigured here? The Lord says there shall be a highway for the remnant of his people, like unto what? Does he say, like as it was in the day when Israel came up out of the land of Babylon? No. "Like as it was to Israel in the day that he came up out of the land of Egypt." At the time the prophet wrote these words the Lord's hand had not been set to recover Israel from the Babylonish captivity. They had never yet been delivered from Babylon, and hence the prophet comparing what shall come after with what has gone before, says there shall be a highway, such as was prepared for the people of the Lord when he brought them up out of the land of Egypt.

Now I wish to refresh your minds with a statement that I have already made two or three times in the progress of this discussion; that there is not a solitary prediction of the restoration of the twelve tribes, but what was made before their restoration from the Babylonish captivity, and that does not, in that event, find its full and entire fulfillment.

I now call your attention to a declaration made by my opponent. He stated that there is no place in the Bible where the words "all nations" mean more than all nations then living. I shall not take issue with him on this point. I would just as lief admit that as not. It is said that all nations shall be gathered before Christ at the time of his coming, and not only they, but the very ones that pierced him are to look upon him also. Not only are they who shall be living at the time of his advent to behold him, but the very ones who thrust the spear into his side. Surely that is plain enough, and I really cannot see why my friend has brought this matter up at all, unless it be in order that he may, cuttle-fish-like, hide himself behind a dark cloud of his own raising, and induce his hearers to lose sight of the great truth so strikingly set forth in the word of God, that "they shall look on him whom they have pierced," in that great day.

Again you were told by my friend that the Greek preposition *eis* may be translated "to," with as much propriety as it can be translated "into." I hold in my hand Bullion's Greek grammar, a work which will not be called in question by my friend as being a work of authority upon all such points as the one before us. We have the definitions of these three Greek prepositions, *eis*, *ek* and *en*. And what does the author here say about the meaning of the preposition *eis?* I will read it to you: "*Eis*—PRIMARY SIGNIFICATION, *to, into, motions from without to within*—the opposite of *ek*." Let us see how *ek* is defined. "*Ek*—PRIMARY SIGNIFICATION, *from, out, out of—motion from within to without*—the opposite of *eis*." Having thus the meaning of these two opposite words before us, let us look at the definition of the third, *en*—an intermediate term between the other two. "*En*—PRIMARY SIGNIFICATION, *in;* with the idea of rest and being contained within." Here then we have, upon the authority of Mr. Bullion, as well as of Liddell and Scott, who define the words in the same way, the preposition *en*, signifying *in*, containing the idea of rest, and also the idea of being within. On the one side of this middle word *en*, signifying *rest within*, we have two extremes—two words signifying motion; one, however, signifying motion from within to without, and the other from without to within —*eis* being defined as the opposite of *ek*, and *ek* as the opposite of *eis*. If *ek* means "out of," then *eis* means "into"—neither more nor less—for *eis* is the opposite of *ek*. Having thus, then, these words and their significations clearly before us, as defined by men who are scholars indeed, we will leave this thought for the present.

I wish to make a remark or two in relation to my friend's criticism in regard to the "ancient of days," and will ask you to go with me to Daniel, 7th chapter. You recollect the position my opponent assumed in regard to the language to be found there. I am going to show you that his leaving out the word "days" is not going to help him any; neither is his adding the letter "s" to the word "ancient." In the 13th verse of the chapter before us, it is stated that they brought "him," *i. e.* Christ, near before another "him," not "them," and that "him" was the "ancient of days." In the next place, you observe that if you add the letter *s* to the word "ancient," so as to make it plural, you are compelled either to throw out the word "him" and make it "them," or else you must throw out the entire phrase and put in one of domestic manufacture. And, my friends, you should be very careful how you give credence to any system of religion that depends for its support on a Bible of domestic manufacture. But how will the passage in question read when amended as the gentleman proposes, by leaving out the word "days," and adding an *s* to the word "ancient"? It will read as follows:

"They brought him near before *them*, and there was given him dominion and glory and a kingdom, that all people, nations and languages should serve him: his dominion is an everlasting dominion, which shall not pass away, and his kingdom that which shall not be destroyed."

On an examination of the language we find it absolutely impossible that the words the "ancient of days," should be applied to the angels or any other beings in the universe than the Eternal himself. The pronoun "him" is used, being in the singular number. But above all other objections stands this, that the moment you apply the term "ancient of days" to the angels, you make the angels give to the Savior this dominion and glory, and this everlasting kingdom, which shall never be destroyed. I think it will puzzle my friend Mr. Stephenson, with all his talent for mystification and special pleading, to show how any one can give to another that which he does not himself possess. I think he knows very well that the angels are not the possessors of all these things. What, then, is the true meaning of all this? The simple idea is, that when Christ ascended to the skies, attended by his angelic escort, the voice of the Eternal Father is heard, saying to him, "Because thou hast loved righteousness and hated iniquity, therefore sit thou on my right hand, until I make thy foes thy footstool." Then it was, after his resurrection from the grave, and his ascension into heaven, that there was given unto him dominion and glory, and a kingdom, that all people, nations and languages should serve and obey him.

I wish, in the next place, to examine my opponent's reading of the 14th verse of the 3d chapter of Joel:

"Multitudes, multitudes in the valley of decision: for the day of the Lord is near in the valley of decision."

Look at the 16th verse of the same chapter:

"The Lord also shall roar out of Zion, and utter his voice from Jerusalem; and the heavens and the earth shall shake: but the Lord will be the hope of his people, and the strength of the children of Israel."

Observe the first clause of the verse before us. "The Lord also shall roar out of Zion and utter his voice from Jerusalem." This was to be at the time of Christ's personal appearing at Jerusalem. His kingdom was to be there established—when that kingdom was set up then Christ would roar out of Zion and utter his voice from Jerusalem.

But the remainder of the verse goes on to state: "But the Lord at that time, will be the hope of his people, and the strength of the children of Israel." Here my opponent must change sides once more. He inquired if we could hope for anything that we already had? At the time here spoken of in the 3d chapter of Joel, we are told that the Lord will be the hope of his people. Now unless a man can hope for what he already possesses my friend is in a very bad situation just here. Do you recollect his asking me, if we already were in possession of the kingdom, why we still professed to be hoping for it? May I not with equal propriety ask him why he continues to hope for all this which is so manifestly fulfilled in the past. In the same manner I might go on and show his inaccuracy in many other passages.

In Hebrews, 5th, 6th, 7th and 8th chapters, Paul describes the priesthood of Christ. My friend admitted that if Christ is now a priest after the order of Melchisedek, he is now upon his throne. Go with me to Zechariah 6th chapter and 13th verse and you will find that "he shall be a priest upon his throne." Then if he is now a priest after the order of Melchisedek, he is a priest now upon his throne. This will speedily settle the entire controversy. What says the apostle Paul in regard to this matter? Speaking of Christ he says in first verse of the 8th chapter of Hebrews, " We have such an high priest, who is set on the right hand of the throne of the majesty in the heavens." And in the 5th chapter and the 10th verse he says of him, that he was "called of God, an high priest after the order of Melchisedek." He does not say after the order of Aaron, but "after the order of Melchisedek." Again we find the same thought presented no less clearly in the 11th verse of the 7th chapter.

"If therefore perfection were by the Levitical priesthood, (for under it the people received the law,) what further need was there that another priest should rise after the order of Melchizedek, and not be called after the order of Aaron?"

Thus far through the whole discussion my friend has viewed Christ as a priest after the order of Aaron and not at all after the order of Melchisedek. But mark the language of the apostle, "If therefore perfection were by the Levitical priesthood what further need was there that another priest should rise after the order of Melchisedek, and not be called after the order of Aaron?" Now Mr.

Stephenson and Paul differ, for Mr. Stephenson makes Christ a priest after the order of Aaron; Paul, after that of Melchisedek. There is not a solitary hint or intimation in the whole Bible of the Messiah being anything but a priest after the order of Melchisedek, but on the contrary, everything that bears upon the matter at all goes to preclude any such idea entirely. Look at the expression before us, and with this plain and clear language in view, I will ask my friend Mr. Stephenson to show us an expression if he can, anywhere in the Bible, showing the Messiah to have ever been anything else but a Melchisedekian priest, from the first verse of Genesis to the last "amen" of Revelations.

But a priest must have something to offer. When he therefore approached the priestly office he offered himself —his own body and blood and he offered it once for all. Now, if Christ is now a priest after the order of Aaron he will have nothing to offer when he shall come again to become a priest after the order of Melchisedek, unless, indeed, my friend would persuade us that he is going to die again. The simple truth is that Christ is not now an Aaronic but a Melchisedekian priest. It follows therefore that there is no other sacrifice needed. But if Christ is yet to enter upon his office as a Melchisedekian priest what is the next offering to be? He must do one of two things—either he must die again in order to provide himself an offering, or he must present the singular anomaly of a priest without an offering the next time he becomes a priest. This whole thought of Christ's filling the office two different kinds of priesthood is sheer nonsense and gross error, having not a word of authority within the lids of the Bible.

The Savior's origin, according to the flesh, engaged my friend's attention to a considerable extent. What was that origin? Answer—It was through David, from the tribe of Judah. Now, the tribe of Judah was prohibited by law from furnishing any one for the priesthood. Christ belonged to that tribe; he could not, therefore, be a priest while on earth. He came from the kingly tribe, and consequently he could fill no order nor office whatever, but one of a kingly nature. Paul says he was of the tribe of Judah, and John says he was "the lion of the tribe of Judah."

## NEG.—J. M. STEPHENSON—NINTH SPEECH.

I wish, in the first place, to notice a few of the more prominent positions assumed by my opponent, and will then pass on to a survey of the subject before us.

He tells us that there is between the lids of the Bible no where a solitary promise on the part of the Almighty to restore Israel a *third time*. In reply to that I would simply remind him, that there has never been to this day a restoration of the twelve tribes of Israel. There is no such statement in the Bible, nor do we find any evidence or record of anything of the kind upon the pages of profane history. The restoration promised—the restoration spoken of by the prophets—is a general restoration of the whole house of Israel. It was only Judah and Benjamin, and a small remnant of the ten tribes that returned from the captivity in Babylon. In the day here spoken of in the 11th chapter of Isaiah, the wolf shall lie down and sleep side by side with the tender lamb, and the leopard shall lie down by the kid, and the calf and the young lion shall feed together, and a little child shall lead them. There shall be nothing to hurt nor destroy in all my holy mountain, saith the Lord, for the earth shall be full of the knowledge of the Lord, as the waters cover the sea. There shall be one wide and universal peace in that day. Then it is in that day "the Lord shall set his hand to recover the remnant of his people which shall be left." "And then shall he set up an ensign for the nations, and shall assemble the outcasts of Israel, and gather together the dispersed of Judah from the four corners of the earth-" This is the 12th verse that I have just read. And then it goes on and enumerates the various nations out of which the remnant of the Lord's people shall be brought up to the land of Palastine. It calls them by their ancient names, Assyria, Egypt, Pathros, Cush, Elam, Shinar and Hamath, and "from the islands of the sea." This is precisely the same thing that is prophesied in Ezekiel, 37th chapter, where the children of Israel are represented as being taken from among the heathen whither they are gone, and gathered in on every side and brought into their own land, and the two nations, Israel and Judah, united into one nation in the land upon the mountains of Israel, never more to be plucked up thence, but to dwell forever in the land, and to be greatly multiplied. And we are told that one king shall rule over them, and that the covenant of the Lord shall be with them for evermore. Here, then, is a promise that has never yet been fulfilled, and which will be at last fulfilled in the restoration of the whole house of Israel to their own land, the land of Palastine; and when once restored to that land, they shall never more be plucked up.

My opponent places a great deal of stress upon the statement that all nations are to be gathered together in the last days when Christ comes. I say amen to that with all my heart. Turn to Zechariah xiv: 1, 2, 13, 14, for the proof: "Behold, the day of the Lord cometh, and thy spoil shall be divided in the midst of thee. For I will gather all nations against Jerusalem to battle; and the city shall be taken, and the houses rifled, and the women ravished; and half of the city shall go forth into captivity, and the residue of the people shall not be cut off from the city. And it shall come to pass in that day that a great tumult from the Lord shall be among them," (referring to the time when all nations shall be gathered together against Jerusalem,) "and they shall lay hold every one on the hand of his neighbor, and his hand shall rise up against the hand of his neighbor. And Judah shall fight, and the wealth of all the heathen round about shall be gathered together, gold and silver and apparel in great abundance." And those who shall survive this tumult in which every mans' hand shall rise against his neighbor, will be smitten with plagues. And after all these nations that have gathered themselves together against Jerusalem shall be overthrown, what shall then take place? "And it shall come to pass," says the 16th verse, "that every one that is left of all the nations which came up against Jerusalem, shall even go up from year to year to worship the king, the Lord of Hosts, and to keep the feast of tabernacles." Joel iii: 1, 2: "For, behold, in those days, and in that time, when I shall bring again the captivity of Judah and Jerusalem, I will also gather all nations, and will bring them down into the valley of Jehoshaphat, and will plead with them there for my people and for my heritage Israel, whom they have scattered among the nations, and parted my land." These are that part of the nations that did not come up against Jerusalem—those of them that staid at home—they shall come up from year to year to worship the King of Jerusalem, and to keep the feast of tabernacles. After Christ's coming, and the overthrow and destruction of the armed hosts of the nations, there shall be a period of probation for those left at home, and the commandment of the Lord will go forth to them from Jerusalem, and they will come up to the holy city to keep the feast and to worship the King.

But the identical men who pierced Christ, my opponent says, are to be there. Did I not refer you to the seventeen nations, the representatives of whom were assembled together at Jerusalem on the day of Pentecost, to whom Peter declared, "Ye have crucified the Prince of Life?"—and did I not show you that that assertion could be no more true, taken in a literal sense, than the expression, "they shall look upon him whom they have pierced." I ask again, did those men to whom Peter was talking personally, crucify Christ? I showed you that these two expressions are to be interpreted in precisely the same manner. Neither of them could be true, taken literally; but just in the same sense, that the men whom Peter was addressing had crucified Christ, the men who shall be living on the earth, the Jewish nation of that day, shall look upon him they have pierced. The men who had personally crucified Christ were of the same nation with those whom Peter was addressing, and the men who personally pierced him belonged to the same nation that they will belong to who shall look upon Christ, "whom they pierced," at his second coming. This is the whole truth in regard to that matter.

The preposition $eis$, as I think I have stated before, is translated by "FOR" one hundred times in King James' translation of the New Testament. George Campbell renders $eis$, in the passages relating to baptism, by "in order to." I have taken pains to note down ninety places in which the preposition $eis$ is rendered into English "FOR." The primary signification of the word is not in all cases applicable, and it is often used with considerable latitude of meaning.

The word "metestesen" which is rendered in the passage quoted by my friend "translated," is twice rendered into English "TRANSLATE," and twice into "CHANGE." Of the latter interpretation we have an example in the 12th verse of the 7th chapter of Hebrews: "For the priesthood being CHANGED, there is made of necessity a CHANGE also of the law." The Greek Lexicon and Englishman's Concordance of the New Testament, also renders it "CHANGE." In the 11th chapter of Hebrews, in reference to Enoch, it is rendered "translated." This passage, and the one quoted by Mr. Russell, are the only two instances in which the word is rendered into English by the word "translate;" and in two instances the same orignal word is translated "CHANGE." A literal translation from the original would read, "Who hath delivered us from the power of darkness, and hath changed us for the Son of his love."

Campbell's translation is good authority with Disciples. Where we read that John baptized in Jordan for the remission of sins, he renders $eis$ "IN ORDER TO," thus: "in order to the remission of sins." He thus renders it in Acts, 2:38, "Repent and be baptized IN ORDER TO the remission of sins." We may translate $eis$ "FOR," or "IN OR-

DER TO," thus: "Who hath translated us for, or in order to, the kingdom."

My opponent seemed to suppose that he had made a splendid point, in reference to the language, "the ancient of days." I think I said distinctly that a celebrated Hebrew scholar, a man fully qualified to give an intelligent opinion on the point, said that the word might be either singular or plural. The word in the Hebrew that occurs in this passage, and that is translated "ancient of days," is not the only word of which the same remark may be made, by any means; ELOHIM is another. In the 26th verse of the 1st chapter of Genesis, we read, "And ELOHIM said, Let us make man in our own image, after our likeness." In the following verse we read: "So God created man in his own image; in the image of God created he him; male and female created he them." Here we have a noun in the plural, and a personal pronoun in the singular used in place of it, and verbs both singular and plural agreeing with it.

In reference to my opponent's statements in regard to what he calls the impossibility of the angels giving the glory and dominion and kingdom to Christ, I would simply say that angels are the power by whose means and through whose instrumentality the great God has been pleased to govern the world. And Paul says, in Hebrews, 2d chapter and 5th verse: "For unto the angels hath he not put in subjection the world to come, whereof we speak?" Here we see it clearly taught that at Christ's second advent, as in the formation and the government of the world thus far, angels will perform an important part. When the Prince of Persia (?) contended with the Angel Gabriel twenty-one days, (Dan., 10:13) he recognized this fact, for he supposed the angel was interfering with his affairs. The intelligent reader of the Word of God can not fail to be convinced that God, while he is the sovereign ruler of the universe, has, always, when he interposed in the affairs of this world, employed angels as his instrumentalities.

But I have not time to notice all the little objections that my opponent throws across the path of truth in this discussion. I cannot conceive what his object is in pursuing such a course, unless it is merely for the purpose of compelling me to consume my time in removing them out of my way, in order that I may not have sufficient leisure to attend to the more material and important parts of the discussion.

I will call your attention, however, to the position he took in reference to his "kingdom"—the Church. In his kingdom there are but three elements,—first, a king; second, subjects; and third, laws. He has no territory, no capital, no cabinet. It is an anomaly among kingdoms. He has shorn it of nearly all the elements of any kingdom that has ever existed, and still persists in calling it a "kingdom." It has no royalty, no cabinet, no civil power. It has no power at all but such as is purely ecclestiastical. It is supremely ridiculous to call such a thing as that a "kingdom."

But my opponent wanted to prove to us that there were subjects submitting themselves to the laws of his kingdom on the day of Pentecost. Peter told the assembled multitudes to repent and be baptized, he says, and they did so, and that proves that they were loyal subjects of his kingdom. But were they Christians before they obeyed? They could not be said to be subjects of his kingdom until they were taken into the church and they obeyed before they were taken in. If to obey the command of Peter to repent and be baptized be made the proof of their loyalty as subjects, it must be shown that they were subjects at the time the command was given. They should have been first made the subjects of the kingdom, and then to given proof of their being loyal subjects afterward.

Let us read the 13th and 14th verses of the 7th chapter of Daniel: "I saw in the night visions, and, behold, one like the Son of man came with the clouds of heaven, and came to the Ancient of days, and they brought him near before him. And there was given him dominion, and glory, and a kingdom, that all people, nations, and languages, should serve him. His dominion is an everlasting dominion, which shall not pass away, and his kingdom that which shall not be destroyed."

Again I ask my opponent this question: Was this prophecy fulfilled on the Day of Pentecost? Did all nations serve and obey Jesus Christ at that time? He has proven that three thousand persons were added to the church under the preaching of the apostles at that time; but were they "all nations?" There is no man nor woman here who does not know better than that. But this is not all that was to occur at that time—the time when the Son of Man came to the Ancient of Days. There was given unto him at that time dominion and glory and a kingdom. Again I ask the question: Was dominion and glory and a kingdom given to him on the Day of Pentecost? and did all nations and people and languages serve and obey?

We have before us, in this same chapter, an account of Daniel's vision of the four great beasts that came up out of the sea, representing four universal empires of the world. The fourth beast was Rome. In the 18th verse it is said that "the saints of the Most High shall take the kingdom (*i. e.* 'the fourth kingdom of earth,' 23d verse) and possess it forever." Was this fulfilled on the Day of Pentecost? Did the saints of God take Rome? and will they possess it forever? On the contrary, Rome took the church and dispersed its broken and shattered elements among the nations of earth. Rome broke in pieces the church, instead of the church breaking Rome.

The prophet said to King Nebuchadnezzar, in explaining to him the vision of the great image that he had seen in a dream: "Whereas thou sawest the feet and toes, part of potter's clay and part of iron, the kingdom shall be divided." He does not say "kingdoms," but "*the kingdom* shall be divided." Only one of the four kingdoms, represented by the four beasts in the vision of Daniel, existed at any one time. They were all universal empires. It does not follow, however, that there was only one kingdom after the kingdom represented by the fourth beast was divided. On the contrary, the very idea of division implies that from that period on there must have been at least two kingdoms. My opponent's point here, as you very well recollect, was that the words," in the days of these kings," Daniel ii: 44, refer to the last rulers of the Roman Empire. I expect to show you that, on the contrary, the demonstrative adjective "these," in the 44th verse, refers to the kings who were to rule over the nations into which the Roman Empire was divided—that it is in their days that the God of Heaven shall set up a kingdom. These kingdoms were to be partly strong and partly weak, as indicated by the fact that while some of the toes of the great image were of iron, part were of miry clay. It is " in the days of THESE kings." The adjective "these" denotes the last in the series of kings. Rome had ceased to be a consolidated empire at the time indicated by the iron and the clay—viz.: when Rome was in its divided state.

Now, when was Rome divided? That nation was in the zenith of its glory at the time of the birth of Christ, and at the day of pentecost. I have in my hand an authentic history, from which I propose to read to you in regard to the time at which Rome was divided, as represented by the toes of iron and clay; after which division the kingdom spoken of in Daniel, 2d chapter and 44th verse, must have been set up. We find in the history of that age no clay mingled with the iron which was so appropriate an emblem of the powerful and despotic empire of ancient Rome, until three hundred and fifty years after the day of pentecost. I will read from page 38 to the close the first paragraph of page 39 of the "History of Revolutions in Europe":

"Constantine the Great, was the first of the emperors that embraced Christianity, and made it the established religion of the state in 324. He quitted the city of Rome, the ancient residence of the Cæsars, and fixed his capital at Byzantium, in 330, which took from him the name of Constantinople. Anxious to provide for the security of his new capital, he stationed the flower of his legions in the East, dismantled the frontiers on the Rhine and the Danube, and dispersed into the provinces and towns, the troops who had heretofore encamped on the borders of these great rivers. In this way he secured the peace and tranquility of the interior, and infused, for a time, a new vigor into the government; but he committed a great mistake in giving the first example of making a *formal division* of the state between his sons, without regard to the principle of unity and indivisibility which his predecessors had held sacred. It is true, this separation was not of long continuance; but it was renewed afterwards by Theodosius the Great, who finally divided the empire between his two sons in the year 395; Arcadius had the eastern, and Honorius the western part of the empire. This latter comprehended Italy, Gaul, Britain, Spain, Northern Africa, Rhetia, Vindelicia, Noricum, Pannonia, and Illyria. It was during the reign of Honorius, and under the administration of his minister, Stilicho, that the memorable invasion of the barbarians happened, which was followed shortly after, by the destruction of the Western Empire."

All the predecessors of Constantine the Great, for three hundred years, had held sacred the unity of Rome. He, dying in the middle of the fourth century, was the first of all the emperors who divided his empire between his sons. Let us read on a little further:

"Several of the Emperors, guided by a short-sighted policy, had received into their pay several battalions of foreigners; and to recompense their services, had assigned them settlements in the frontier provinces of the empire. Thus the Franks obtained, by way of compensation, territories in Belgic Gaul; while similar grants were made in Pannonia and in Thrace, to the Vandals, Alans, Goths, and other barbarians. This liberality of the Romans, which was a true mark of weakness, together with the vast numbers of these troops which they employed in their wars, at length accustomed the barbarians to regard the empire as their prey. Towards the close of the year

406, the Vandals, the Suevi, and the Alans, sounded the tocsin of that famous invasion which accelerated the downfall of the Western empire. The example of these nations was soon followed by the Visigoths, the Burgundians, the Alemanns, the Franks, the Huns, the Angles, the Saxons, the Heruls, the Ostrogoths, and the Lombards. All these nations, with the exception of the Huns, were of German origin."

There you have the first division of the Roman empire that ever was made. It was after that time that the God of heaven was to set up his kingdom which was to endure forever.

My opponent says a stone and mountain, in prophetic language, mean the same thing; and both the stone and the mountain mean his kingdom, the Church. But you recollect that it says the stone became a great mountain. Now is it true that a stone and a mountain are the same? Is not one local and the other universal? To talk of a mountain becoming a mountain, is sheer nonsense. How is his kingdom to grow into a mountain if it was a mountain at first?

In reference to the 110th Psalm, I have proved over and again, that the Father will make Christ's foes his footstool, by investing him with authority to reign over them. For you to make a footstool for me, and for me to place my foot upon it, are two entirely different things. It is the Father who is to prepare Christ's footstool, but it will be left for Christ himself to put his foot upon it, by subduing and treading down his enemies. The Father makes the foes of Christ his footstool by making him their ruler, and then shall he rule them with a rod of iron —he shall dash them in pieces as a potter's vessel.

The adverb "until" limits the time specified. Speaking of Christ, the Apostle Peter said, (Acts, 3d chapter, 21st verse,) "Whom the heavens must receive *until* the times of the restitution of all things." If I should say that you should detain me here untill to-morrow, would you understand from that that I was to stay here forever? Certainly not. If Christ were to stay forever at the right hand of the Father in heaven, the Apostle would not have used that word "until." It shows beyond a shadow of doubt that the time is to come when he will remain there no longer. Read the 23d verse of the 15th chapter of 1st Corinthians:

"But every man in his own order: Christ the first fruits; afterward they that are Christ's at his coming."

I demonstrated beyond the shadow of a doubt that the same original word is used in both cases, thus: "Christ the first fruits AFTER they that are his at his coming." "AFTER the end." He does not inform us how long after his coming the *end* will be, but he assures us that it will be subsequently to his coming, and the resurrection of the righteous dead. He also tells us that it shall cover the period of his reign, until he shall have subdued or destroyed all his enemies, the last of which will be death. At the end, after this event, he delivers up the kingdom to his Father.

The great event here spoken of is to come to pass, when? "After" his coming. This period may as well therefore embrace a thousand years as any other period. How long is to be the period in which Christ shall reign? What is to be the duration of his kingdom? Turn to 2d Peter, 3d chapter: "One day with the Lord is as a thousand years, and a thousand years as one day." Here we have the "day of the Lord" as a thousand years. Paul, in Acts, 17th chapter and 31st verse, says: "He hath appointed a day in which he will judge the world by that man whom he hath ordained." "He has appointed the day." How long will Christ rule the world independently? See Revelations, 20th chapter and 4th verse, where John tells us that he saw thrones, and they sat upon them; and that judgment was given unto them; and that he saw the souls of them that had not worshiped the beast nor his image; and they lived and reigned with Christ *a thousand years.* And in the 6th verse, the same period is repeated:

"Blessed and holy is he that hath part in the first resurrection: on such the second death hath no power, but they shall be priests of God and of Christ, and shall reign with him a thousand years."

The "day of the Lord" will be a period of a thousand years. At the commencement of that period all the righteous dead will be brought up out of their graves, and all the righteous living will be changed, and they will "live and reign with Christ a thousand years."

---

## AFF.—P. T. RUSSELL.—TENTH SPEECH.

Things new and wonderful are rapidly accumulating upon our hands as we approach the end of the discussion. Let us look at some of them.

In the first place I direct attention to my opponent's allusion to Acts 3d chapter, where the language occurs: "Whom the heavens must receive," or, if you please "retain" "until the times of the restitution of all things, which God hath spoken by the mouth of all his holy prophets since the world began." Now, it so happens, that one of Israel's old prophets did speak of the doing away of the present heaven and the present earth, and the ushering in of new heavens and a new earth—and if it is a fact that the adverb "until" marks the time during which Christ shall be retained at the right hand of the Father, then it is certain that he is to be retained there until the new heavens and the new earth shall be brought in; and if he is retained there until that time he cannot reign, nor can my friend Mr. Stephenson or those who are of the like faith reign with him a thousand years before that time.

Another point which my friend attempted to make in his last speech on yesterday, I think it was—it was in relation to the new Jerusalem—the city which John says he saw descending from God out of heaven, and which the righteous are to enter. He had the righteous all inside as you recollect, and the wicked all without. Inside all are kings. As I asked before, I repeat the inquiry—who are those kings that are without the walls to reign over? For although the gates of this city were to remain open night and day, yet at the same time no righteous person within was to be permitted to go out, nor was any of the wicked who were without to be permitted to go in, and that being the case I cannot see how they are going to rule the rebels who are without the gates of the city, any more than the United States government could have ruled the rebellious people of the South, if they had not sent their armies down there into the rebellous states to compel them to submission.

In Revelations 21st chapter and 27th verse it is said that "there shall nowise enter into it," that is to say into the city; "anything that defileth, neither whatsoever worketh abomination or maketh a lie." Here it is evident that none of the outsiders can come into the city at all. Turn now to the 3d chapter of Revelations and let us see if any of the *insiders* can get out. I will read the 12th verse of the chapter or a part of it. "Him that overcometh will I make a pillar in the temple of my God, and *he shall no more go out.*" And yet the doors of the city stand open all the time. Why are the doors open thus continually and yet neither the wicked can get in to drive the righteous out, nor the righteous can get out to whip the wicked in? There is a good deal of improbability in this view of the city to say the least.

And now we must pass to look at some other matters. In his last speech my friend seems to have misinterpreted what I said in regard to the priesthood of Christ. I did not deny that Christ was the great anti-type prefigured by the Aaronic priesthood, but I did deny that he was filling any other priestly office than that of a Melchisedekian priest. The Aaronic priesthood was typical of the Melchisedekian, which Christ is now fulfilling at the right hand of the majesty on high.

I now desire to give a brief survey of the entire subject which is before us. In the first place the elements of a kingdom are clearly and repeatedly presented to our minds throughout the entire range of those portions of Holy Scripture which bear upon this subject. The "throne" of God is often spoken of. The Lord is said to be "the king, eternal, immortal and invisible." The original kingdom and dominion of God was overthrown so far as the government of our race was concerned when sin came into the world. The divine government being thus overthrown by the rebellion of his subjects, a medium of communication was afterward opened up between the throne and the rebels, God taking the initiation in the negotiations and keeping the intercourse up through his prophets down to the coming of Christ. From the day of Pentecost down, every man who accepted of salvation upon the terms of the gospel has been in the kingdom of God. Before that time the righteous upon earth occupied a position not unlike that of a citizen of the United States, who was down in Rebeldom during the war, where there was no government in force.

John the Baptist and the Apostles came in the capacity of provost marshals whose business it was to take men out from under the dominion of the rebellion against the authority of God, and admit them to the privileges of citizenship in his kingdom on the terms of obedience. During the rebellion the provost marshals were continually employed in taking men out from under the ban of the rebellion, upon their taking the oath of allegiance to the government—in other words "translating" them into the government of the United States, although that government was not yet re-established in an organic form within the limits of the territory in which they lived. In the 31st verse of the 21st chapter of Matthew, Christ told some of the chief priests and elders of the Jewish people, that the publicans and harlots would go into the *kingdom of heaven* sooner than they. And again, in the 23d chapter and 13th verse he says:

"But woe unto you, scribes and Pharisees, hypocrites! for ye that shut up the kingdom of heaven against men;

for ye neither go in yourselves, neither suffer ye them that are entering to go in."

The Savior was at that time preparing to set up his kingdom in an organic form and all men were commanded to come into it — to take the oath of allegiance to Heaven's King and become subjects to Messiah's reign, and many were obeying the call—and hence the language to which reference has just been made. That kingdom was shortly to be set up—Christ was to be a priest forever after the order of Melchisedek—such a priest he could not be unless he was a king upon his throne. Paul declares that he is now a priest after the order of Melchisedek; consequently he is now, and was when Paul wrote, upon his throne — the throne of his kingdom which was established on the day of Pentecost, at the city of Jerusalem—when the law was proclaimed from Mount Zion—when thousands submitted themselves to that law and were made subjects of the kingdom of our Lord Jesus Christ. Remember the fact that I have repeatedly challenged my opponent to produce a single chapter or verse anywhere within the lids of the Bible, going to show that Christ was to be a priest after the order of Melchisedek at any other time than when he was upon his throne. He admitted that Christ must be a high priest after the order of Melchisedek when he is upon his throne. Paul says he is now such an high priest—therefore as a natural consequence he is now upon his throne. There is no intention in the Bible anywhere of his ever being a priest of the order of Melchisedek, except when he is on his throne.

We now call your attention to some other matters in connection with this important subject. Turn, if you please, to the first chapter of the epistle of James, and first verse. I will read this verse for the sake of the bearing it has upon the question of the identity of the "twelve tribes" of whom the apostle makes mention, with the true followers of Christ.

"James, a servant of God and of the Lord Jesus Christ,

to the twelve tribes which are scattered abroad, greeting."

Here James is writing to something which he calls "the twelve tribes," and says to them in the verses which immediately follow, "My brethren, count it all joy, when you fall into grievous temptations; knowing this, that the trying of your faith worketh patience."

Take this language in connection with Acts, 26th chapter, 6th and 7th verses:

"And now I stand and am judged for the hope of the promise made of God unto our Fathers: unto which promise our twelve tribes, instantly serving God day and night, hope to come: for which hope's sake, King Agrippa, I am accused of the Jews."

Here once more I put the plain, simple question to my opponent—Is literal Israel serving God now day and night? Were they doing so when James wrote? Were they doing so when they were clamoring for the life of the Savior, and imbruing their hands in the blood of his disciples? Certainly not. The apostle, however, is talking about an Israel that was serving God truly. The 11th chapter of the epistle to the Romans has been brought forward. Let us examine it, and see what is said there about literal Israel:

"What then? Israel hath not obtained that which he seeketh for; but the election hath obtained it; and the rest were blinded. (According as it is written, God hath given them the spirit of slumber, eyes that they should not see, and ears that they should not hear;) unto this day. And David saith, Let their table be made a snare, and a trap, and a stumbling block, and a recompense unto them: let their eyes be darkened that they may not see, and bow down their back alway."

If literal Iisrael is ever to be restored, then this language cannot be true. You will have to go to the other end of "always" before you can find the time when they are to be brought back from their rebellion and apostacy. In the 11th verse, immediately following the passage I have read, Paul says:

"I say, then, Have they stumbled that they should fall? God forbid: but rather through their fall salvation is come unto the Gentile, for to provoke them to jealousy."

Here we have already presented the final fall of literal Israel. Why did they fall? Because of unbelief. How can they be brought back? They must first believe in the Messiah before they can receive favor at his hand. Literal Israel is spoken of as falling away from God, through unbelief. See what a contrast there is between literal Israel as presented to us here, and the Israelite indeed, as described in Romans, 2d chapter, 28th and 29th verses:

"For he is not a Jew which is one outwardly; neither is that circumcision which is outward in the flesh: but he is a Jew which is one inwardly: and circumcision is that of the heart, in the spirit, and not in the letter; whose praise is not of men, but of God."

Here we have literal Israel, Israel after the flesh, contrasted most strikingly with something else called by the same name, Israel.

And while we are on this point, go with me to 1st Corinthians, 10th chapter and 18th verse:

"Behold Israel after the flesh: are not they which eat of the sacrifices partakers of the altar?"

Here we have a vivid contrast between Israel after the flesh and Israel after the spirit. Here we have a stubborn fact, showing that two wholly dissimilar things are named "Israel."

The time of Israel's possession of the land of Palestine, as promised by the prophets, at the time when they were driven out of it by the Roman power, and from that time, or till the second coming of Christ, will be the "times of the Gentiles." By the Gentiles will the land of Palestine be trodden down until the day when he comes, and then, at the time of his coming, the elements shall melt with fervent heat, the heavens are to be rolled together as a scroll, and the world, and all the works that are in it, are to be burned up. The earth and heavens—this whole visible frame is to pass away with a great noise, and a new heaven and a new earth are to take the places thereof, and in the midst of the new earth is to be formed the city of the Great King—the great capital of the Kingdom of the saints, which comes down from God out of heaven. It is not to be formed upon this sin cursed globe of ours.

Let us follow this thought a little further. Go with me to the 24th chapter of Matthew, and 29th verse:

"Immediately after the tribulation of those days shall the sun be darkened, and the moon shall not give her light, and the stars shall fall from heaven, and the powers of the heavens shall be shaken."

This plain and unequivocal language, that right after the "tribulation of those days" the wonders and signs that are but a prelude to the end of all things upon this sublunary sphere, shall display themselves, cuts off all idea of the intervention of the period of a thousand years. Read the next verse:

"And then shall appear the sign of the Son of man in heaven: and then shall all the tribes of the earth mourn, and they shall see the Son of man coming in the clouds of heaven with power and great glory."

The tribulation of the days here spoken of is to roll on in an unbroken current until the son of man shall come again, "without a sin offering unto salvation," and all the holy angels with him, to reward every man according to his works. We have therefore good reason to declare the truth boldly, and without the fear of successful contradiction, that the times of the Jews, the times within which they were to possess the land of Palestine, expired when they were driven from that land by the Roman power, and that the Gentiles will continue to have control of that land as they now have, until the second appearing of the Son of man to judge the quick and the dead, when all the tribes of the earth shall mourn, when "they shall see the Son of man coming in the clouds of heaven with power and great glory."

Look at the language of the 37th verse, and on:

"But as the days of Noe *were*, so shall also the coming

of the Son of man be. For as in the days that were before the flood they were eating and drinking, marrying and giving in marriage, until the day that Noe entered into the ark, and knew not until the flood came, and took them all away; so shall also the coming of the Son of man be."

All the rebels against God in that day, will find to their sorrow, that instead of having another thousand years probation, as my friend supposes, they will be swept as with the besom of destruction. Mark the force of the comparative term "so"—As it was in the days of Noe, "so" shall it be when the Son of man shall come.

Pass now in confirmation of this truth to the testimony of Luke as contained in his Gospel, 21st Chapter and 25th verse and on:

"And there shall be signs in the sun, and in the moon, and in the stars; and upon the earth distress of nations, with perplexity; the sea and the waves roaring; men's hearts failing them for fear, and for looking after those things which are coming on the earth: for the powers of heaven shall be shaken. And then shall they see the Son of man coming in a cloud with power and great glory."

Having thus this matter placed before us in the same form in which we find it in the other place, I ask on the testimony before us, what is the conclusion that we must draw from all the premises? Let us follow the Apostle on a little further:

"And when these things begin to come to pass, then look up, and lift up your heads; for your redemption draweth nigh. And he spake to them a parable; Behold the fig tree, and all the trees; when they now shoot forth, ye see and know of your own selves that summer is now nigh at hand. So likewise ye, when ye see these things come to pass, know ye that the kingdom of God is nigh at hand. Verily I say unto you, This generation shall not pass away, till all be fulfilled."

Here is represented the final consummation of all things —the time when the Son of man shall come in his glory, and all the holy angels with him; and when he shall sit upon the judgment seat, and all the slumbering nations of the dead shall rise from their tombs and stand before him; when he shall separate the righteous from the wicked as a shepherd divideth the sheep from the goats; and shall say to those upon his left hand: "Depart, ye cursed into everlasting fire prepared for the devil and his angels," but to those upon his right hand, "Come, ye blessed of my Father, inherit the kingdom prepared for you from the foundation of the world." And while the word of God thus teaches us what shall take place when Christ shall come, Paul adds that he shall judge the living and the dead *at his appearing*—not a thousand years afterward, but *at his appearing*. What must be the conclusion drawn from the matters thus placed before us?

When John the Baptist came preaching the kingdom of God, he said that kingdom was *at hand*. The Savior, just a little while before his crucifixion said the same thing. Now if the position which my opponent assumes is true, then it is plain that the second coming of Christ, and the date of the setting up of his kingdom must have been equally distant in point of time when Christ was upon earth, and when John preached, "Repent, for the kingdom of heaven is at hand." And in the light of this truth I again put to my opponent this plain and simple question: Could Christ and John tell the truth and say that the kingdom of heaven was *at hand*, if it were contemporaneous with the second coming of Christ? The kingdom of God—the same identical kingdom spoken of in Daniel, 2d Chapter and 44th verse, was "nigh at hand," while we know very well that the second advent of Christ has not yet taken place, though eighteen centuries and more have elapsed since the time when Christ and Paul said the kingdom of heaven was "at hand."

## NEG.—J. M. STEPHENSON.—TENTH SPEECH.

It is said that "flesh and blood shall not inherit the kingdom of God." If the kingdom of God, as my friend Mr. Russell claims, is the Disciple church, then that text does not tell the truth, for there is a great deal of flesh and blood in the Disciple church as we all know. Are they not composed of flesh and blood like other mortals?

How do my friend and his brethren read the Lord's prayer? Do they say "Thy *church* come," instead of "Thy kingdom come?" If they cannot offer such a prayer they are not consistent in their faith. These are a few of the more striking beauties of Discipleism. They can utter this prayer in a place where they have no church.

One of the positions assumed by my opponent was, that if it be true that Christ is to be retained at the right hand of the Father until the time of the restitution of all things, then he must remain there during the period of a thousand years mentioned by John in Revelations, and as a natural result he cannot reign upon the earth during that time. He should read it "until the *times* of the restitution of all things," and not until the "time." He is to come in the times of the restitution of all things—amidst the closing ages of the world's history. My opponent is a shrewd schemer. I think he would be a very good debater if he only had the truth upon his side.

He said again that he did not deny that Christ was an anti-type of Aaron. Now he acknowledges it. Hence we can have a priest in heaven, although we have none now upon the earth.

He says that Christ is the anti-type of Melchisedek according to the language of Zechariah, vi: 12–14.

"And speak unto him, saying, Thus speaketh the Lord of hosts, saying, Behold the man whose name is The BRANCH; and he shall grow up out of his place, and he shall build the temple of the Lord; Even he shall build the temple of the Lord, and he shall bear the glory, and shall sit and rule upon his throne; and he shall be a priest upon his throne; and the counsel of peace shall be between them both." This does not say he will be a priest upon his throne in heaven, but when he shall be a priest upon his own throne.

Turn now if you please to the 33d chapter of Jeremiah, 15-18 verses, and notice what is there said upon that point. See what the prophet says about the righteous Branch.

"In those days, and at that time, will I cause the Branch of righteousness to grow up unto David; and he shall execute judgment and righteousness in the land. In those days shall Judah be saved, and Jerusalem shall dwell safely: and this *is the name* wherewith he shall be called, The LORD our Righteousness.

"For thus saith the LORD: David shall never want a man to sit upon the throne of the house of Israel; neither shall the priests the Levites want a man before me to offer burnt offerings, and to kindle meat offerings, and to do sacrifice continually."

Either that righteous Branch is to be here upon the earth, to occupy the throne of David, and execute judgment and justice in the land, or the prophet was laboring under a mistake when he wrote this chapter. Christ is now upon his Father's throne and not upon his own throne. His own throne is the throne of his father David. When he shall come again he shall sit upon David's throne, and from that time on David shall never want a man to sit upon his throne—and a priest to offer sacrifices. Such are the harmonious teachings of the word of God.

My friend has a sort of a military kingdom — and the Apostles occupy the position of so many provost marshals empowered to bring back by force the recreants to their allegiance and compel them to take the oath of allegiance. My friend occupies the position of a chaplain in this military organization of which he speaks. Let me ask you Mr. Russell, are you going to pray God to direct the cannon balls when you fight for the kingdom —is that the way you are going to "take" the fourth kingdom, and possess it? Christ said, "My kingdom is not of this world—if it were then would my servants fight. In this age and dispensation the servants of Christ do not fight in that way. His servants will not fight until his kingdom is set up. The word which is here translated "world" is kosmos, and signifies "order" or "arrangement." The Savior meant simply that his servants would not fight to maintain the present civil government or "arrangement,"—kosmos means in this place simply the Roman Empire. When the kingdom shall be given to Christ then will his servants fight to maintain it. My friend Mr. Russell is in the wrong position.

My opponent says the Jews are to be trodden down and oppressed by the Gentiles until the second coming of Christ. "Until." That implies at once that a time will come when they will cease to be trodden down. Christ, in the 23d Chapter of Matthew tells the Jews that they shall not see him henceforth *until* the time shall come when they shall say, "Blessed is he that cometh in the name of the Lord." This language shows that the time is coming in which the Jewish people shall repent and turn unto the Lord, and the Lord will accept their repentance and restore them to all that they have lost through their disobedience and rebellion against God.

My opponent tells us that, as it was in the days of Noah and of Lot, so shall it be in the end of the world. The bible calls Noah alone, of all who were saved, a righteous person. It does not appear that any other member of his family deserved the name. The record does not state what their character was. Of Lot's family, we know that he alone was righteous, for his wife was so disobedient that God turned her into a pillar of salt, and the subsequent conduct of the two daughters shows very clearly that they were far from being righteous. Hence, three-fourths of those who were saved from the destruction of Sodom were unrighteous, and of those who were saved from the deluge, six-sevenths were, for anything we know to the contrary, no less righteous than the others. It was for the sake of Noah himself that he was allowed to build the ark. The conduct of his son Ham demonstrates that he was not righteous. Hence, if so many persons were saved from destruction by the deluge, and so many from the destruction of the cities of the plains, who had all of them been unrighteous up to that very time, may we not infer that a portion of the wicked will be spared when Christ shall set up his kingdom, and that many shall submit to his authority out of the nations of the earth, and shall go up to the city of Jerusalem every year to worship the King, and to keep the Feast of Tabernacles?

Will the great God come to earth? In the 2d Chapter of Titus occurs the language: "Looking for the blessed hope, and the glorious appearing of the great God and our Saviour Jesus Christ." The original term here rendered "glorious" is "doxe." It occurs in the New Testament about one hundred and sixty times, and in one hundred and forty-five times out of that number it is translated into English by the noun, glory, and in only seven by the adjective as it is in King James' translation in the passage just read. It should be rendered, "Looking for that blessed hope, and the glory of the great God and our Savior Jesus Christ." In only seven of all the hundred and sixty instances in which it occurs in the New Testament, is this word rendered "glorious," in all the rest it is translated "glory."

Why is the book of life opened, as John says in Revelations, 20th chapter and 12th verse, in connection with the other books out of which the dead were judged when they came up from the sea and from Hades? I will answer the question in the light of God's word. Christ said, "The words that I speak unto you shall judge you at the last day." He sent his disciples into the world, telling them, "Go preach the gospel unto every creature. He that believeth and is baptized, shall be saved, but he that believeth not shall be damned." Damned because they would not believe. The names of those who believe and obey, and afterwards apostatise, are to be blotted out from the book of life. See Rev. 3:5. Christ says, addressing his church, "He that overcometh, the same shall be clothed in white raiment; and I will not blot out his name out of the book of life." Thereby implying that the names of apostates shall be blotted out of the book of life. When a person, through faith and obedience, becomes an heir of immortality, his name is recorded in the book of life; (i. e. eternal life) but when he apostatizes from the faith, or its obedience, he forfeits his title to eternal life, and when he shall have been judged he will be remanded back to death, from which he shall never be raised. The book of life is to be used in judging apostates. When a man apostatizes, his name is to be blotted out of the book of life. At what time? I answer—When he stands before God in judgment, and that will be at the end of a thousand years after the coming of Christ. The book of life is to be opened and apostates are to be judged out of that book, preparatory to blotting out their names. It does not necessarily follow, however, that the faithful who overcome are to be raised from the dead and judged at the same time. Their accounts were previously settled. They are not the subjects of litigation. They, as has been demonstrated, will be raised and rewarded a thousand years before.

Suppose I keep accounts in a ledger, and at the end of a hundred days one class of men have paid their accounts —show debits and credits equal; another class have accounts that show only debts for a long period of time, and no credits at all. Now when I shall close my books and settle up, what class of customers will be the subjects of litigation? Certainly those who have not paid up—those who are delinquent. Will it follow that when I balance my books, and give a receipt in full to those who have paid, that I will, at the very same time, prosecute all those who are delinquent? Not at all. The time of proceeding against them may be deferred until the end of a year. So shall it be when Christ shall come to judge the world. In the 20th chapter of Revelations John says:

"Blessed and holy is he that hath part in the first resurrection: on such the second death hath no power, but they shall be priests of God and of Christ, and shall reign with him a thousand years."

Hence, those who shall be accounted worthy shall be raised from their graves, and shall live and reign with Christ a thousand years, while all the rest of the dead are slumbering there, and shall not be brought to account for a thousand years.

If the kingdom is the church, why is the kingdom held out to us in the teachings of Christ and his apostles as the great inducement to obedience?

Christ came into the world to save sinners, says Paul. By what motive did he save sinners? Answer—through the motive power of a promised kingdom. Addressing a multitude of sinners, he called upon them to reform. What great inducement did he hold out as a reason why they should reform? Answer—"And at that time Jesus began to preach, and to say, Repent, for the kingdom of heaven is at hand."—Matt., 3:17. Christ was annointed for the specific purpose of preaching the gospel—Luke, 4:18. What was the subject of the gospel which he everywhere preached? Answer—the kingdom. Listen to the testimony of Matthew: "And Jesus went about all the cities and villages, teaching in their synagogues, and preaching the gospel of the kingdom."—Matt., 9:35. Listen also to Luke's testimony. He says: "And it came to pass afterward, that he went through every city and village, preaching and shewing the glad tidings of the kingdom of God."—Luke, 8:1. Christ, in the 16th chapter of Mark, and 15th and 16th verses, commands his apostles to herald to the world a proposition, upon which the salvation or condemnation of a responsible world is suspended. What was the import of that great and sublime proclamation? Answer—the gospel of the kingdom. He commissioned his apostles to go into all the world and preach the gospel to every creature, with assurance that "he that believeth and is baptized shall be saved, but he that believeth not shall be damned." In Matt., 24:14, he predicts the fulfillment of this great gospel commission in the following significant language: "And this gospel of the kingdom shall be preached in all the world for a witness unto all nations;" thus teaching, that the gospel which he commissioned his apostles to preach in all the world, and by which he proposed to save or condemn the world, was the gospel of the kingdom.

But he commanded his apostles to tarry at Jerusalem until they should be endued with power from on high, Luke, xxiv: 49. They obeyed the divine injunction, and Peter just ten days after the ascension of our Lord to heaven, stood forth on the day of Pentecost and preached the first gospel sermon under this great commission—the motive power of which was the fulfillment of the oath and covenant of God in placing Christ upon David's throne. He says at the 30th verse of the 2d chapter of Acts, when speaking of David: "Therefore being a prophet and knowing that God had sworn with an oath to him that, of the fruit of his loins, according to the flesh, he would raise up Christ to sit upon his throne." That Peter does not mean the Father's throne here as my opponent affirms, is evident from the Oath of God recorded in the 132d Psalm and 11th verse. "The lord hath sworn in truth unto David; he will not turn from it; of the fruit of thy body will I set upon thy (David's) throne."

In the 8th chapter of Acts and 5th verse, we are told that Philip went down to the city of Samaria, and preached Christ unto them." At the 12th verse of the same chapter those who heard Philip preach, inform us relative to just what he preached. Listen to their testimony: "But when they believed Philip preaching the things concerning the kingdom of God and the name of Jesus Christ, they were baptized both men and women."

In Acts, 20: 25, Paul tells us what had been the whole theme of his preaching, up to that time—covering a period of more than twenty years of his ministry; he says, addressing for the last time those beloved brethren among whom he had labored for years, "And now behold,—know that you all among whom I have gone preaching the kingdom of God shall see my face no more."

The kingdom of God was the great theme of all his

preaching during the last two years of his life. The following is the closing history of this great man's labors. "And Paul dwelt two whole years in his own hired house, and received all that came in unto him. Preaching the kingdom of God, and teaching those things which concern our Lord Jesus Christ, with all confidence, no man forbidding."—Acts, xxviii: 30.

The apostle James presents a future kingdom as the great theme of promise and hope to the people of God, thirty years after the day of Pentecost in the following language.

"Hearken, my beloved brethren, Hath not God chosen the poor of this world rich in faith, and heirs of the kingdom which he hath promised to them that love him?"

Peter in a general epistle written more than thirty years after the day of Pentecost, holds out an abundant entrance into the kingdom as the subject of hope.

"Wherefore the rather, brethren, give diligence to make your calling and election sure: for if ye do these things, ye shall never fail: For so an entrance shall be ministered unto you abundantly into the everlasting kingdom of our Lord and Savior Jesus Christ."

From these testimonies we learn that in all the preaching of Christ and his apostles before and after the day of Pentecost, the kingdom is held out as the motive power of the gospel.

## AFF.—P. T. RUSSELL—ELEVENTH SPEECH.

I will in the first place call your attention to the allusion made by my friend to history. In the book of Daniel, 2d chapter, we have this language: "In the days of these kings,"—not "those kings"—but "In the days of these kings shall the God of heaven set up a kingdom." The demonstration "these" always points to those persons or things that are more near, and the demonstration "those" to such as are more remote. There are but four kings spoken of in connection with this language. But my friend, when he turned to the history, left the consideration of this passage, and turned to the 9th of Daniel, where occurs the account of Daniel's vision of the four beasts; and then he had a little to say about the ten toes of Nebuchadnezzar's great image.

Let us examine a little into my friend's argument from history. Between the years 457 and 483, not only was the Roman empire subverted, but ten different kingdoms arose out of its ruins. These ten kingdoms are represented in Daniel, 7th chapter and 24th verse, by the ten horns that arise from the heads of the four beasts. In the beginning of the sixth century, the little horn subverts three of these kingdoms. As it was in the days of "these kings," according to Daniel, 2d chapter and 44th verse, that the kingdom of the God of heaven should be set up, it must have been either in the time of those mentioned in Daniel, 2d chapter, or those mentioned in Daniel, 7th chapter, and emblematized by the ten horns. If it was in the days of these ten kings, it must evidently have been before the time when three of the ten kingdoms were subverted; for the three being subverted, you have but seven left, and consequently the prophet is wrong in saying that it shall be "in the days of these kings."

It was to be "in the days of these kings." Where are the Huns to-day? Where are the Goths or the Vandals? Where are the Ostragoths or the Visigoths? The province of Andalusia, in Spain, is the spot where the old Vandal empire once stood. The nation has been blotted out of existence for centuries. They were, but are not. Where are the Lombards to-day? Echo answers—"where?" What was once the site of the ancient kingdom of Lombardy, is now but a province belonging to another nation. What has become of the ten nations into which the empire of ancient Rome was divided? The waters of oblivion roll over them.

My friend attaches a great deal of importance to his new rendering of Titus, 2d chapter and 13th verse. If his translation of that passage is correct, then there is no evidence at all that either the Father or the Son is going to appear, but only their glory. He would have it read, " Looking for the appearing of the glory of the great God and our Savior Jesus Christ." They both remain behind the blue curtain, and only their glory shines out.

There is one assertion of my friend which I must examine with some little care. He told you that the apostles never taught the doctrine of a present kingdom. Whether they did or not, one thing is very certain, and that is this: they taught the doctrine of a kingdom in which they represented themselves and their brethren as being at that very time. If the gentleman will show me a place in the New Testament where the apostles teach the idea of a kingdom in which they say that they or their brethren in Christ, a thousand or two thousand years hence, will be, then I will assent to his statement that they did not teach a present kingdom. But if the apostle said, " We receiving " (using the present tense) " a kingdom which can not be moved "—and if he told the truth, and if that kingdom is the same kingdom which is described in Daniel, 2d chapter and 44th verse, and which is called an everlasting kingdom—then I claim that not only did the apostles teach and preach a present kingdom, but that kingdom is now, and ever since the day of pentecost has been, set up upon the earth. Paul says that he and his brethren were receiving that kingdom and enjoying it. He says also that he and his brethren had been translated out of the power of darkness into the kingdom of God's dear Son.

Let us now turn and look at some other matters in connection with this subject. I want to present to your minds two or three contrasts. In my friend's last speech he took the ground that the proclamation made by John the harbinger, " Repent for the kingdom of heaven is at hand," and the preaching of the apostles under the great commission, " Go preach my Gospel to every creature," were identical. I assent that John the harbinger could never preach that the kingdom of heaven was at hand as a witness. No person can be presented as a witness, nor can anything be introduced as evidence, unless that person or that thing is in such a position that it can be made the subject of examination. John preached the kingdom of heaven as coming—as not yet come, but nigh at hand. But the apostles preached the gospel of the kingdom as a thing that had already come, for they preached it as witnesses. They preached the gospel "for a witness unto all nations." In the 16th and 17th verses of the 1st chapter of the Epistle to the Galatians, Paul teaches the fact that he was a witness of the kingdom into all men.

Let us pause here for one moment, and ask the question—How were the disciples to preach the gospel of the kingdom? Were they to preach it as something that was yet to come? or as something that has actually come? Were they to preach it as something away off in the dark vista of the future, or as something that was accessible at that very time—accessible to them that heard? Hear one of the same witnesses I have brought up before—what says the apostle? "Who hath delivered us from the power of darkness, and translated us into the kingdom of God's dear son?" Does a consistent preacher preach about anything in the same manner that he writes about it? He certainly does. The apostles wrote about the kingdom of heaven as a thing that had already arrived—a thing that was actually in being at the time. They preached the kingdom as an institution that was set up on the earth by the God of Heaven for the benefit, and for the salvation, of the very men to whom they preached; they represented the doors as being open to receive them, and they were commanded to enter in.

I defy my opponent to find one solitary place in the New Testament where, after our savior's ascension on high, any divinely inspired writer or speaker, has ever written or said, that the kingdom of heaven is *nigh* or *at hand*. Before that time they did thus speak. Why is it that this is the case? The answer is simply, that up to that time Messiah had not been crowned king. When he ascended upon high he received his kingdom. His apostles were directed to go and preach the gospel to every creature, but to tarry at Jerusalem until they were enendued with power from on high. Then came the day of Pentecost; the apostles received power from on high, and went forth preaching the gospel of a present kingdom. From that time forward we hear no more about the approach of the kingdom of God. The simple reason is, that it had already come.

I want now to inquire into the cause of another striking contrast. Why were different reasons given for the command to repent before and after the date I have mentioned? John the Harbinger, commanded the people to repent, "for the kingdom of heaven is at hand." This points forward to that event as coming—as future. After the resurrection and ascension of the Messiah, they point backward to the same event. In Acts, 17th chapter, and 30th and 31st verses, we read:

"And the times of this ignorance God winked at; but now commandeth all men everywhere to repent: because he hath appointed a day, in the which he will judge the world in righteousness, by that man whom he hath ordained, whereof he hath given assurance unto all men, in that he hath raised him from the dead."

Here we have a direct, perfect and complete contrast presented between the reasons assigned before and after Christ's resurrection from the dead. On the one side they are commanded to repent because the kingdom of heaven is at hand; on the other, because God has appointed a day wherein he will judge the word in righteousness. Here we have an insurmountable difficulty in the way of my friend. John said repent for one reason, the gospel says repent for another, and very different reason.

Mr. Stephenson told you that God now governs the world through the instrumentality of angels. For the sake of the argument let us suppose that to be true—admitting it and taking the Bible to be true, at the same time my position still stands uncontroverted and incontrovertable. For Peter says in his first epistle, chapter 3d and in the last verse:

"Who is gone into heaven, and is on the right hand of God; angels and authorities and powers being made subject unto him."

If "angels authorities and powers," all are subject to Christ as a natural consequence God has made him the king supreme; for according to my friend, the angels govern the world and they are under him. This being so Christ is not only king supreme *de jure*, but he is also king *de facto*, over all and above all. Turn and read in connection with this thought, Colossians 1st chapter 15th, 16th and 17th verses.

"Who is the image of the invisible God, the first born of every creature; For by him were all things created, that are in heaven, and that are in earth, visible and invisible, whether they be thrones, or dominions, or principalities, or powers: all things were created by him, and for him: And he is before all things, and by him all things consist."

We find Jesus Christ then in the first place as God in heaven, seated at the right hand of the majesty on high, and clothed with the glory which he had with the Father before the world was, and angels authorities and powers made subject unto him. These words express everything that has power in all the universe and all it includes is made subject unto him. Hence Mr. Stephenson and the apostle taken conjointly place my affirmative position on a rock against which the gates of hell or hades cannot prevail. In this view of the case as well as in any other, Jesus Christ is at this very time upon his throne. He is at this very time KING OF KINGS AND LORD OF LORDS.

Let us now take that text in the 110th Psalm in which we find God the Father addressing the Son and saying to him, "Sit thou on my right hand until I make thy foes thy footstool." This language is afterward quoted and commented on seven or eight times by the Apostle Paul who declares that he is to remain there until all his foes are subdued. The last foe that will be subdued is death, and death cannot be subdued until all ruling power is taken away from him by the resurrection of the last human being that shall have entered death's domain—and hence as a natural consequence the Son is to remain at the right hand of the Highest, until the final consummation of all things. Then Paul, right in close connection with what I have just quoted says that Christ is then to give up the kingdom to God, even the Father, that God may be all and in all.

## NEG.—J. M. STEPHENSON—ELEVENTH SPEECH.

My opponent refers again to Col., 1:13. I have shown by the authority of Greenfield, and the Englishman's Greek Concordance, that the original word rendered "translated," signifies "to change," and may just as appropriately be applied to a repentance or change of mind; that it is translated CHANGED just as often as it is TRANSLATED. I have also shown that the preposition $\varepsilon \iota \varsigma$, rendered "INTO," is translated into the preposition "FOR" in our common version, near one hundred times. Also that it is translated "in order to," by Campbell, which ought certainly to be good authority with my opponent. The following is the Dioglote translation of this verse: "Who hath delivered us from the dominions of darkness, and CHANGED us for the kingdom of the Son of his love."

Mr. Russell persists in quoting Rev., 1:9, to prove that Christians are already in the kingdom. The following translation of Wakefield's, removes all objections to the view I have presented: "I, John, your brother, and sharer with you in enduring the affliction of the kingdom of Jesus Christ, was in the island called Patmos on account of the word of God, and the testimony of Jesus Christ."

On Friday my opponent had Hades vocal with the cries of the damned; on the next day he had Hades giving up the dead in it. During the debate on the first question, Mr. Russell denied the power of God to raise dead men; but in the discussion of this question he has earth, sea, and Hades giving up their dead, and they stand as living, organized men in judgment. His conversion is almost too sudden. I have not much confidence in death-bed conversions.

Angels administer the government of God only in times of special interposition on the part of the great God, as in the flood, and the destruction of the cities of the plains. They will execute his judgment upon the guilty nations. Christ is the head of all things, Paul says to his Church, (Eph., 1:22). This is Paul's explanation: Christ's power is purely ecclesiastical. He has no civil power or regal glory now. He is the head of the new creation, not the old. As has been shown, when he comes as King of Kings and Lord of Lords, then he will be the head of all principalities and powers. The world to come will then be put in subjection to him.

Mr. Russell does not pretend that we have come to the literal Mount Zion, or the Son of God. In fact it has been proved that when the last great whirlwind of revolution shall sweep from their base all the kingdoms of the world, that at that time the people of God will receive a kingdom which cannot be moved. That is the point of time designated by the apostle when the saints shall come to Zion, and shall receive an immovable kingdom.

My opponent takes the position that Israel, which will be saved when Christ comes, will be spiritual Israel; that there is no promise for literal Israel. Paul says, "For if the casting away of them be the reconciling of the world, what shall the receiving of them be, but life from the dead?"—Rom., 11:15. Again he says, that partial blindness had happened to Israel until the fulness of the Gentiles should be come in; and so all Israel should be saved.—Rom., 11:25, 26. And at the 28th verse, he says, "As concerning the gospel, they are enemies for your sakes: but as touching the election, they are beloved for the Fathers' sakes."

I have answered my opponent's position, that the kingdom was at hand in the days of Christ and his apostles. I have shown that "at hand" means the next event in the ordinal relation of events, as well as in relation to space or time.

As has been shown, five successive and universal empires are in God's appointed order to occupy the earth. These are Babylon, Media-Persia, Greece, Rome, and the kingdom of God. Had Christ and his apostles preached during the existence of Babylon, they could not have preached the kingdom of God at hand, because Media-Persia was to be the next in God's order. Had they preached during the existence of this kingdom, they could not have preached the kingdom of God at hand, because Greece was the next in order. Had they preached during the existence of Greece, they could not have preached the kingdom of God at hand, because Rome was the next in order. But inasmuch as they preached during the existence of the last universal kingdom which shall precede the kingdom of God, they could very appropriately proclaim the kingdom of God at hand,—that is the next in the order of God's appointment.

But Christ in the 21st chapter of Luke having commenced with the encompassing of Jerusalem with armies, traces down the series of events through the destruction of Jerusalem, and the dispersion of the Jews among all the nations of the earth—and still on he stretches out the great line of prophetic events until the times of the Gentiles are fulfilled. Taking his stand point at the closing up of the times of the Gentiles, he then gives the signs of his second advent, and says to the generation that shall live contemporaneous with these signs and the coming of Christ: "So likewise ye, when ye see these things come to pass, know ye that the kingdom of God is NIGH at hand."—Luke xxi: 31. Compare with verses 20–28. At the commencement of this dispensation the kingdom of God was simply at hand, but when the last signs evidence its close Christ authorizes us to say that the kingdom of God is nigh at hand. I have urged this objection to my opponents position in almost every speech, and without attempting to reply he continues to affirm that the kingdom of God is never spoken of as being at hand after the day of Pentecost. Mr. Russell agrees with me that Luke traces the history of the Jews down to the close of the present dispensation and the last signs of Christ's personal coming. He and I agreed upon this point this morning. He was afraid I would take the position that the "days of vengeance" which Christ foretold, at the terminus of which these signs should appear which would evidence to the generation that should see them, that the kingdom was near at hand—was fulfilled at the destruction of Jerusalem, and thus prove that the kingdom was only at hand at the destruction of Jerusalem. How with this admission he can affirm that the kingdom is never said to be at hand after the day of Pentecost I cannot understand. Mr. Russell refers again to Micah 4th and also Isaiah 2d, and applies them to the day of Pentecost. With his own position that the last verses of the third chapter of Micah which preceed the verse he quotes, received their fulfillment at the destruction of Jerusalem—how he can carry back the future tense of the verb to a time anterior to the destruction of Jerusalem I cannot conceive. Having just described the destruction of Jerusalem the prophet adds: "But it shall come to pass in the last days." Does the verb SHALL, denote the past or future tense of the verb? Answer—the future always. How then can he carry back the tense of a verb which denoted future time at the destruction of Jerusalem, and make it designate an event which transpired forty years previously? It is not in the power of language to help my opponent out of this dilemma. The last of the future days at the destruction of Jerusalem, are the last days of the dispensation which succeeded the destruction of Jerusalem. And when the signs of the last days are seen we may know that the kingdom of God is nigh at hand. This is a nail in a sure place, driven by the master of assemblies.

Rome became a universal empire at the battle of Actium, thirty years before the Christian Era, and continued so for over three centuries and a half. It was in the zenith of its glory at the advent and during the preaching of

Christ and his apostles. Rome continued a consolidated and undivided empire, as represented by the unmixed iron, until the middle of the fourth century. The event did not occur which eventuated in the division of Rome until Constantine transferred the seat of empire from Rome to Constantinople in A.D. 330. After his death the Roman empire was divided into what is denominated Eastern and Western Rome by Theodosius the Great, who finally divided the empire between his two sons in the year 395. It was subsequently divided into ten kingdoms as was demonstrated by history.

My opponent has not noticed these historical arguments against his position, that the stone smote the image on the day of Pentecost, notwithstanding he promised to do so. He knows they are utterly irreconcilable with his position. Daniel says, " whereas thou sawest the iron mixed with clay, the kingdom shall be divided." The mixing of the clay with the iron denotes the division of Rome. The stone smites the image after the commingling of the iron and clay; (for it strikes the image upon the feet, which *are of iron and clay*) therefore it does not smite the image until after its division in the last of the fourth century, for, as has been demonstrated, Rome was not divided until A. D. 395. These invulnerable objections will go to the reader of this discussion without an attempt on the part of the affirmative to answer them. Daniel does not say how many toes there are, but he does say in the days of these kings. Daniel uses the singular noun kingdom before the clay is mixed with iron; but after this mixture of clay with iron—which he says denotes the fourth kingdom in its divided state—he uses the plural noun kings. As has been shown, king and kingdom are used synonymously; if, therefore, the God of heaven had set up his kingdom on the day of Pentecost, it would have been in the days of this king, for no two of these four kings (kingdoms) existed contemporaneously. It was king, or kingdom, before the division, but kings, or kingdoms, after. And according to Daniel the God of heaven will set up a kingdom in the days of the last mentioned kings, which, according to Daniel and history, will be the kingdoms represented by the iron and the clay—Rome divided. The demonstrative adjective *these* designates the last kingdoms in the series; these were the last kingdoms of the Roman empire, in their brittle—their iron and clay condition—partly strong and partly weak—just as the kingdoms in the Roman territory are to-day. The first evidence of the collision between the stone and image is the utter destruction of the image, when all the kingdoms represented by it shall pass as chaff before the winds of the summer's threshing floor. Was this fulfilled on the day of Pentecost? Has it since been fulfilled? It has not. Has the church broken to pieces and ground to powder the fourth kingdom of earth? Just the reverse has been true. The fourth kingdom broke Christ, the head of the church, in pieces, and destroyed all the visible church he had on earth, and scattered the remnant all over the world. In its Pagan and Papal forms it held dominion over, and persecuted, and destroyed by hundreds of millions, the church and the people of God. Constantine converted the church to the world, and thus prepared the way for the great apostacy, which arose upon the demoralization and almost extinction of christianity from the earth. My opponent agrees with me that the coming of Christ in the clouds of heaven to reward every man according to his works, will be the second advent at the close of the present dispensation. At that time, Anti-Christ, with all his leagued hosts, will be destroyed. Then the world of ungodly will be destroyed. But they will be the living nations of earth. I have proved from the 14th chapter of Zachariah, Joel 3d and Revelations 16th, that all nations will be gathered in Palestine when Christ shall come in power and great glory. I have also shown that all nations which will be overthrown in the last great battle, will be the kings, potentates, armies and navies of the world, as represented by the beast, the dragon and the false prophet—that a remnant of all nations will be left at home, and be organized into the kingdom of God.

I have also shown that the 110th Psalm will meet its fulfillment in the coming age, when Christ shall be a king upon his throne, and rule in the midst of his enemies; when the rod of God's strength—Christ—shall wound the heads—kings of earth—and fill the valleys with their dead bodies. He will then—according to Zech., 6th chapter, and Jer., 33d chapter—be a priest upon his throne, to execute judgment and justice in the earth; and from that time forward, David shall never want a man upon his throne.

The Father, as has been shown, makes Christ's foes his footstool, by investing him with authority to rule over them, when, according to the 2d Psalm, he will break the incorrigible in pieces as a potter's vessel, and extend mercy to all who put their trust in him.

My opponent, in his last speech, acknowledged that the everlasting kingdom will not be set up until Christ's second advent. Thus he has yielded the whole point at issue. During the entire discussion, he has argued that the kingdom spoken of in Daniel, 2d and 7th chapters, will never pass away—never be moved—will stand forever; that the terms used to measure their duration are the strongest in the Bible to denote an absolute eternity. And all these positions have, from the commencement, been conceded by our side. And now, in his next to the last speech, he yields the whole point. I do not know whether to be glad or sorry at this accession to our ranks. As before stated, I have not much confidence in death-bed conversions.

## AFF.—P. T. RUSSELL.—TWELFTH SPEECH.

I wish to notice one other matter contained in the argument of my friend. He thinks that the words "at hand" mean next in order—the nearest of a series of events. Admitting this to be true, there is no avoiding the conclusion that my affirmative proposition is correct.

Let us connect this with some other matter, and see what the result will be. The language before us reads, "In the days of these kings shall the God of Heaven set up a kingdom." The reference is to the kings mentioned in Daniel, 2d chapter. These four kingdoms are all that are included within the language, "In the days of these kings;" and the last of the four kingdoms mentioned was the Roman empire. The Roman empire, as we have seen, was subverted soon after the beginning of the Christian era; consequently, it must have been before that time that the God of Heaven should set up his kingdom. In harmony with this is the language of the 4th chapter of Micah: "It shall come to pass in the last days, that the mountain of the Lord's house shall be established in the top of the mountain, and it shall be exalted above the hills, and people shall flow unto it"—referring, evidently, to the time when should come to pass the events spoken of in the 3d chapter immediately preceding this language. In harmony with this is the language of Isaiah, 2d chapter:

"And it shall come to pass in the last days, that the mountain of the Lord's house shall be established in the top of the mountains, and shall be exalted above the hills; and all nations shall flow unto it."

In both these instances the words used are last days, plural, and not last day singular. The voice of Inspiration, speaking through Peter on the day of pentecost, said, "This is that which was spoken by the prophet Joel, And it shall come to pass in the last days, saith God, I will pour out of my spirit upon all flesh, and your sons and your daughters they shall prophesy. Your young men shall see visions, and your old men shall dream dreams." Peter, speaking under divine inspiration, quotes from the prophet Joel, to show that what they were then witnessing was the fulfillment of his prophecy as to what should take place in the last days.

This, then, is the point of time that is marked by the words "last days." If it be not so, then the Holy Spirit made a mistake; and not only the Holy Spirit, but Christ also; for he said, a short time before his death, that he would send the Holy Spirit, as Joel had prophesied he would pour it out in "the last days," and thus sanctioned the idea that the period called by the prophets "last days," was the period in which the wonderful manifestation witnessed on the day of pentecost occurred. My friend had better be cautious how he deals with the plain teachings of divine inspiration.

There can be no doubt that the kingdom spoken of in Daniel 2d chapter and 44th verse was set upon in the days of the Imperial Cæsars, if we have succeeded in establishing the fact that it was to be set up in their days according to the prediction of the prophets. I have shown you, that in that time namely on the day of pentecost, the king was already crowned—that angels, authorities and powers were made subject unto him. I have shown you that at the day of pentecost the law went forth from Zion, and the word of the Lord from Jerusalem —that subjects by the thousand submitted to that law— and here we find everything essential to a kingdom actually existing at that time. The kingdom therefore was "set up" or "established" on the day of pentecost.

The little stone that was cut out of the mountain without hands, became a great mountain. It grew and expanded until it filled the whole earth. The stone is the emblem of Christ's kingdom. Either it must increase now or it never can increase at all. Its growth and expansion must take place beyond all question while the human race are still in a state of probation—and we have found that in the light of the Bible there can be no such idea entertained as that there will be a state of probation after Christ shall come, for we are there taught that he shall judge the quick and the dead at his coming, and not a thousand years subsequently to that coming. It being therefore clearly established that the kingdom of Christ shall grow, and it being further established that it can only grow in a state of probation, it follows, as a natural consequence, that his kingdom is now set up, and that it is not to be set up when Christ shall come again. If set up then it could never increase. If established in a state of probation it is fitly emblematized by the little stone cut out of the mountain side without hands, which grew and increased until it became a mighty mountain and filled the whole earth.

My opponent objected, that Christ is not on his throne at the present time. I think I made it quite clear, with the aid of my opponent that Christ is now upon his throne. He admitted that Christ is now upon his throne, if he is now a priest after the order of Melchisedek, and we proved by the Apostle Paul that Christ is now a priest after the order of Melchisedek—consequently we have proven that Christ is at this very time upon his throne. We challenged Mr. Stephenson to show that there is a solitary sentence in the word of God where Christ is represented as being any other kind of a priest than a priest after the order of Melchisedek, and he has utterly failed to do so. We have shown from the word of God itself that Our Lord and Savior Jesus Christ was not only a priest, but also an high priest—that he was not only an high priest, but an high priest forever after the order of Melchisedek, consequently being an high priest now after the order of Melchisedek he is now upon his throne. The language to which we cited you in Hebrews 5th, 6th, 7th and 8th chapters is entirely conclusive upon this point. The whole matter was admitted by my friend in admitting that if Jesus Christ is now a priest after the order of Melchisedek he is now upon his throne. That is the order of his priesthood forever. He never will be any other kind of a priest than that.

Having shown that Christ is not a king *de jure* merely but a king *de facto*, angels, powers and authorities being subject to him, and all power in heaven and earth being placed in his hands, and that by him and to him are all things created that are in heaven and earth visible and invisible, let us look around us once more.

We find that the very highest possible titles applied to the Savior and all powers in heaven and earth declared to be subservient to him. They give to him the power of a supreme ruler. It is declared by the Eternal himself that every knee shall bow and every tongue confess his authority. It is said of him that he is to sit on the throne of David. To this I reply that David never had a throne in his own right. You may read in Chronicles that Solomon sat on the throne of the Lord in the place of his father David. It was only David's throne by right of occupancy. Christ the son of David is now sitting upon David's throne; that is to say upon the throne of which David's throne was a type. He is seated at the right hand of the majesty on high—at the right hand of the Father where he has been ever since he ascended upon high, and where he will be until death is despoiled of all his power by the resurrection from the dead of every human being that has ever been in death's embrace.

Let us look once more at the idea of the growth of this kingdom. Go to Isaiah 9th chapter where it is said, "To us a child is born, unto us a son is given—and the government shall be upon his shoulder, and his name shall be called Wonderful, Counsellor, the Mighty God, the everlasting Father, the Prince of Peace; And of the increase of his government and peace there shall be no end."

This increase of the kingdom of Christ is shadowed forth by a grain of mustard seed planted in the earth. and again by the leaven which a woman took and hid in three measures of meal. The mustard seed grew until it became a great tree, and the birds of the air came and lodged in its branches. The leaven leavened the whole lump with which it was mingled. Such was to be the growth and increase of the kingdom of Jesus Christ, as shadowed forth in the parable, and by the voice of prophetic inspiration before the day of Pentecost. On that day, in accordance with the prophecies of Micah and Isaiah, the word of the Lord went forth of Zion, and the law from Jerusalem—the assembled multitudes heard the gospel of the kingdom—many of them believed, and in the same day there were added to the church three thousand souls. They were delivered from the power of darkness and translated into the kingdom of God's dear Son.

I willingly let my friend, Mr. Stephenson, have the word "changed," in the passage, instead of the word "translated" into the kingdom. They were "changed," if you please. We have already given you what we thought was a very full and satisfactory explanation of the meaning and force of the Greek preposition *eis*. I showed you the authority of one of the best Greek scholars in the world, that its legitimate signification is "into."

That is the primary, direct and literal meaning of the word, and according to the universally acknowledged rule of translation, we must take that meaning to be the sense in which the word is intended to be understood, unless there are circumstances which positively forbid. There are no such circumstances in the way here. The sense will be complete and the sentence perfectly symmetrical, if we render the word *eis* by its primary and direct equivalent, the English preposition "into." Rendering it thus, these persons were translated out of the power of darkness, and they were translated into the kingdom of God's dear son. These three thousand souls, added to the one thousand and twenty who composed the church of our Lord Jesus Christ up to that time, made the whole number of subjects of the kingdom, when the sun went down on that eventful day, three thousand one hundred and twenty souls. Thus already the kingdom had begun to increase. A little further on a miracle of healing is wrought. A man lame from his birth is found in the temple, walking, leaping, and praising God. Peter and John seizing upon the opportunity presented to them, preached the gospel of the Son of God, and a great multitude of them that heard, believed, "And the number of men," as we learn from Acts, 4th chapter and 4th verse, "was about five thousand." The kingdom is still upon the increase, and now within a few days after the day of Pentecost, eight thousand three hundred and twenty souls have become its willing subjects. A little further along in the sacred narrative we learn that great multitudes were obedient to the faith. The subjects of the kingdom are no longer counted by thousands, but they are "great multitudes." And from Jerusalem the glad tidings of salvation went into all Judea and Samaria, and all Asia. It swept over Europe, and at length has crosséd the broad Atlantic, and throughout the length and breadth of the new world men and women are being brought out of the power of darkness and translated into the kingdom of God's dear Son. Such is the process by means of which the prophecies in relation to the growth and increase of Messiah's kingom are being now fulfilled.

By and by, after the close of the period in which we are now living, the period designated for the growth of the kingdom of the Messiah upon earth—by and by a different condition of things will transpire,—a condition of things to which our Savior had reference, in the language so often quoted in your hearing:

"But as the days of Noah were, so shall the coming of the Son of man be. For in the days that were before the flood, they were eating and drinking, marrying and giving in marriage, until the day that Noah entered into the ark, and knew not until the flood came, and took them all all away: so shall also the coming of the son of man be."

My opponent had a good deal to say about Noah's wife and family being saved without any statement by the inspired historian that they were righteous; but I do not see fit to pay any attention to that kind of play. The comparison made by our Savior was simply with reference to the one idea of a probationary state subsequent to the time of his second coming. As in the days of Noah the wicked were cut off without a single hour of probation, so should it be when the son of man should come. Noah and his family having entered the Ark, the hand of Omnipotence closed the door, and after that, those who were without the ark could no more have got into it, and those inside could no more get out. Just so will it be when the beautiful city, the New Jerusalem, shall come down from God out of heaven; the saints of God will go out no more forever, no will the dogs and sorcerors, and abominable that are without, be allowed to go within the gates; but each shall remain eternally fixed in that condition in which they are found in the second coming of our Lord and Savior Jesus Christ.

Let us now glance for one moment at some of the evidence upon this point. Go again if you please, to Matthew 25th chapter and 31st, 32d and 33d verses.

"When the Son of man shall come in his glory, and all the holy angels with him, then shall he sit upon the throne of his glory; And before him shall be gathered all nations; and he shall separate them one from another, as a shepherd divideth his sheep from the goats; And he shall set the sheep on his right hand, but the goats on the left."

Take in connection with this the language to be found in 2d Thessalonians, 1st chapter, 7th 8th, and 9th verses.

"And to you who are troubled rest with us, when the Lord Jesus shall be revealed from heaven with his mighty angels, in flaming fire take vengeance on them that know not God, and that obey not the gospel of our Lord Jesus Christ; Who shall be punished with everlasting destruction from the presence of the Lord, and from the glory of his power."

When is this to take place? For an answer take the following verse:

"And with all deceivableness of unrighteousness in them that perish; because they received not the love of the truth, but they might be saved."

If the judgment of the quick and dead and the reward of the righteous as well as the punishment of the wicked does not take place at the time of Christ's second advent, then it is perfectly clear that there must be yet two distinct comings of Christ yet in the future; for at one future appearing that is all to take place. There can not be as my friend claims, a thousand years of probation after Christ's second advent unless he is to come a third time—and at that third appearing judge the quick and dead, rewarding every man according to his works. But as we have no intimation whatever in the Bible of any third coming of Christ, and as in the very nature of things that cannot be expected we are forced to the conclusion that at that very time when Christ shall appear, the period of probation for every human being will be at an end—he that is holy shall be holy still, and he that is filthy shall be filthy still.

In perfect keeping with this thought we find the language of the 110th Psalm where the Father addresses the Son saying to him: "Sit then on my right hand until I make thy foes thy footstool." The idea of making the foes of Christ his footstool, and that of the destruction of the wicked from the presence of the Lord and the glory of his power are one and the same—they both refer to the ultimate punishment of the wicked after the final judgment. We have time and again shown that one of the enemies that is to be destroyed—one of the foes that is to be put under the feet of the redeemer is death. We have shown you that death cannot be destroyed—that death cannot be be put under the feet of the Eternal Son until it has lost all ruling power—that death cannot lose all its ruling power until the last human being shall be brought out from under death's dominion by the resurrection — hence, as the resurrection and judgment the reward of the righteous and the punishment of the wicked are to take place when he comes—he cannot be expected until the final consummation of all things—until the last loud trump shall reverberate through heaven. And, says Luke and Matthew, when you shall see the signs of his coming, lift up your heads, ye saints of the Most High, for your redemption draweth nigh. Then shall Christ's kingdom come in its triumphant and everlasting state, when there shall be no more increase, no more conversions, but all shall remain forever as it is. And here the language of 2d Timothy 4th chapter and 1st verse, weaves into my argnment most appropriately where the Apostle says that Christ shall "judge the quick and dead at his appearing and kingdom." Then, at his appearing and kingdom, when he shall have put down all rule and all authority and power—when he shall have put all his enemies under his feet—then shall he deliver up the kingdom to God even the Father that God may be all and in all.

## RECAPITULATION.

Paul says: "When he (God) bringeth again (margin) the first-begotten into the world, he saith, And let all the angels of God worship him." Heb. i: 6. When, according to David, in Psalms, xxii: 27, 28: "All the ends of the earth shall remember and turn unto the Lord; and all the kindreds of the nations shall worship before him; for the kingdom is the Lord's, and he is governor among the nations"—then, and not till then, will every knee bow and every tongue confess. When one like the Son of Man comes with the clouds of heaven, and there is given him glory and a kingdom, and all dominions shall serve and obey, then will all principalities and powers be made subject to Christ. Paul tells us that all things shall be put under Christ in the world to come. Heb. ii: 5-8. But were all things put under Christ on the day of Pentecost? Have they ever been thus subject to him in the world's history?

The word *throne* signifies regal power. God owned David's and Solomon's throne upon earth, but neither David nor Solomon ever owned God's throne in heaven. Christ makes a marked contrast between his Father's throne and his own throne. Rev. iii: 21. He is now upon his Father's throne; but when he comes again he will receive his own throne. Matt. xxv: 31.

If the church is the kingdom, will that increase to all eternity? The Douay Bible renders it—"of his kingdom and the INCREASE OF PEACE there shall be no end." When peace is added it will be an endless peace. The stone, the grain of mustard seed, and the leven, represent the kingdom of Israel restored, and the mountain the full grown tree, and the three measures of meal represent the nations of earth that shall be added to the kingdom of Israel and constitute the dominion.

That a remnant of all nations will have probation for one thousand years, after the advent of Christ, has been proved beyond the shadow of a doubt. That the wicked, who will be destroyed, are the assembled nations in Palestine, has also been demonstrated by the Word of God.

Death, as has been shown, ceases its ravages with the immortalization or destruction of the last mortal man. This will be the case when the last sinner shall experience the second death; then death and hades will be destroyed or cease to be.

According to Dan. 2d and 7th, the everlasting kingdom of God is to be upon the earth. When the kingdom of God shall have come, and his will shall be done on earth as in heaven, then the closing doxology may be sung: "Thine (the Father's) is the kingdom, the power and the glory forever. Amen." But this everlasting kingdom is upon the earth, where the will of God shall be done, as angels do it in heaven.

It has been shown, in reply to the arguments of the affirmative:

1st. That Col. i: 13 only teaches a change in order to the kingdom, and not *present possession* of the kingdom.

2d. That Rev. i: 9 only teaches that John was a fellow sufferer with all Christians on account of the kingdom, and not *in* the kingdom.

3d. That men are not come to the literal Mount Zion, or Judge, or Mediator, or General Assembly—church of the first born—not who are in heaven, but whose names are enrolled in heaven; that the kingdoms of earth are not yet removed out of the way; and that, therefore, we do not receive the kingdom in fact, but by *faith;* that we receive an immovable kingdom when all those things spoken of become realities, and not before.

4th. That Christ and his apostles preached the kingdom of God as at hand—the next kingdom in the series of five universal kingdoms, as Daniel foretold; and that Christ tells us, in Luke, the 21st chapter, when the signs of the times evidence the near approach of Christ the second time, that we may know that the kingdom of God is nigh at hand. My opponent has not met this objection to his position, and can not meet it.

5th. That Paradise, instead of being in a river in heaven, will be within the holy city—New Jerusalem located upon the earth to which the mortal nations will bring their glory and honor; and that it belongs to the world to come—the future age—the third heaven and earth, and not the present.

My opponent has not noticed the evidence adduced to prove that the New Jerusalem—the throne of God and the Lamb—Paradise, the tree and River of Life—will be upon the earth where the nations are, and these nations will be in a mortal and probationary state.

The following insuperable objections to my opponent's position will go to the reader unanswered:

1st. That, at the close of the present dispensation, the kingdom of God, so far from having been established eighteen hundred years ago, will only be near at hand.

2d. The kingdom, instead of being the church, is *offered to the church* as the future reward of obedience, all through the teachings of Christ and his apostles before and after the day of Pentecost.

3d. That the rich can not enter into the kingdom; that little children shall be in the kingdom; that the kingdom is not of this world—age; that it is through much tribulation that we enter the kingdom; that flesh and blood can not inherit the kingdom; that the kingdom is to be established at the second coming of Christ and the judgment of the living and the dead—when God shall reward his servants, the prophets, and those that fear his name, small and great; that the saints are invited to inherit the kingdom—prepared for them when the world was founded—when he shall come to earth, and all nations be gathered before him; and that the kingdom spoken of in Daniel, ii: vii, *will be the everlasting kingdom, and will be located upon the earth—never to be removed, but to stand forever.* Hence, when once established upon earth, it must remain there through the endless ages of eternity. My opponent has acknowledged the issue upon this point.

To recapitulate the affirmative argument:

1st. I have demonstrated that the original dominion of the whole earth was offered to Adam as the kingdom of God; that, in case of obedience, Adam would have been God's regal representative upon earth; that in Paradise would have culminated the power and glory of God's universal kingdom upon earth; that from thence his laws would have radiated for the government of the world; that God offered Adam his everlasting kingdom upon earth upon condition of obedience; that Adam failed to comply with these conditions and lost the glorious privilege of ruling the world in righteousness; that the same lofty position was offered the second Adam, and upon the same conditions: that the second Adam proved loyal in every respect; and that, therefore, the kingdom and dominion offered our great Primogenitor will be given to him. This glorious position is implied in the bright promise of hope for man which followed Adam and Eve as they turned their back upon the fiery guarded gates to go out into the earth where the curse blazed before them —that the seed of the woman should bruise the serpent's head. Christ is the promised seed of the woman. That the serpent is the symbolic representative of the kingdom of men, is evident from Rev. xx: 1–3. The original word rendered *bruise*, signifies to crush or kill. He who shall kill the world's last great representative, will, of course, have a conqueror's right to his dominion. Christ will chain this power for one thousand years, and then utterly and forever destroy him. Having thus hurled the serpentine representative from the throne of universal empire, he will take the kingdom and dominion of the whole earth. That the original dominion of earth will be given to Christ, is evident from his sublime description of his second advent, radiant with the glory of the Father, with all his holy angels as his glittering cohorts. "Then shall he sit upon the throne of his glory, and before him shall be gathered all nations. Then shall the King say to them on his right hand, Come, ye blessed of my Father, inherit the kingdom prepared for you from the foundation of the world."

What kingdom was prepared for man when the world was founded? A kingdom beyond the bounds of time and space? The Church? No! Go back with me to the time when earth's foundations were laid—when the morning stars in sweet concert sang, and all the sons of God shouted for joy, and learn what kingdom was *then* and *there* prepared for man.

The Elohim said, "Let us make man, * * * and let them have DOMINION over ALL the EARTH."—Gen., 1:26. Hence the original purpose of God concerning man and earth—that Adam and all the obedient shall inherit his everlasting kingdom upon earth—will be carried out through the second Adam instead of the first.

Again, the deluge rolled its majestic waves over earth's loftiest mountains, and wrapped in the watery sheet of death the old world, with all its guilty millions; while Noah and his family, the germ of a mighty empire, was borne in the ark of salvation into the new world. Time rolled on, until Nimrod, the mighty hunter, anticipated the future purpose of God in laying the nucleus of a mighty empire, which should prefigure the universal kingdom of God upon the face of the whole earth. Time rolled, on until the angelic messenger was sent to select the only man upon earth intellectually and morally adapted to the purpose of God. His name was Abram. God brought him into the land of Canaan, and changed his name from Abram to Abraham, so that it should fitly represent his future position as the father of a multitude of nations. He then, as has been abundantly proved, made an everlasting covenant with him and his son and grand-son, Isaac and Jacob, that he would give to them and their seed an everlasting inheritance in the land of Canaan, from the river of Egypt to the great river Euphrates. He also promised, that through Abraham, Isaac and Jacob, and their unit seed, all the nations of the earth should be blessed.

It was also shown, from the testimony of Stephen, that God having brought Abraham into that very land, had not given him any inheritance in it, notwithstanding he had promised to give it to him and his son.—Acts, 7:4, 5; and by Paul, that Abraham, Isaac and Jacob died as heirs without receiving the things promised—Heb., 11:9-13; and that therefore, before these promises, backed up by the oath of God, can be fulfilled, they must be raised from the dead, qualified in nature and life to hold an incorruptible and everlasting inheritance. It was also proven by the apostle Paul, that the seed allied with Abraham, Isaac and Jacob, in these glorious promises, are Christ, and all that are Christ's.—Gal., 3:16, 29; and that this everlasting covenant not only pledges the great God to give Abraham and his seed (Christ, and all who are Christ's,) an everlasting inheritance in the land, but the imperial position of the world's dominion. Paul, in his commentary upon these promises, says, "For the promise that he (Abraham) should be heir of the world, was not to Abraham or his seed, through the law, but through the righteousness of faith."—Rom., 4:13. Thus, when heirship shall be merged into possession, Christ and all his people will be the joint rulers of the world, with all nations as their subjects, and the earth upon which these nations dwell as the locality of their kingdom.

Again, after the deliverance of Israel from Egyptian bondage, and their wonderful passage through the desert into the promised land; after the four hundred years, during which God governed them through the seventy judges; after the unrighteous reign of Saul, God selects David from the sheep-cote to be his royal representative upon his throne and kingdom. David's throne and kingdom were the throne and kingdom of God. David was God's legal representative upon earth. Just before David's death, the prophet Nathan was sent to make an everlasting covenant with him concerning the everlasting perpetuity of his throne and kingdom. (See 2d Sam., 7:12-17; 1st Chron., 17:11-17.) David said in the last words he ever uttered, that God had made an everlasting covenant with him, ordered in all things and sure, and that this was all his salvation and his desire. (See 2d Sam., 23:1-5.)

In the 110th Psalm, the Great Eternal testifies in reference to the *nature*, subject and duration of this covenant. He says that he has sworn unto David, his servant, and will not turn from it—that his covenant snall stand fast forever. Then in reference to this everlasting covenant, he says, "Thy seed will I establish forever." And in reference to the position of this royal seed, he says, " Also I will make him my first-born higher than the kings of earth;" that is, I will make him the imperial ruler of the world.

This will be verified when the Son of God shall be seen riding upon his victorious horse, having upon his head many crowns—the insignia of his title to universal empire—while from his crimsoned vesture shall gleam forth the lofty title: "King of Kings and Lord of Lords." He will then be higher than earth's kings and potentates. Still the testimony of the Almighty goes on: "His seed also (Christ) will I make to endure forever, and his throne as the days of heaven. My covenant will I not break, nor alter the thing that has gone out of my lips. Once have I sworn by my holiness that I will not lie unto David. His seed shall endure forever, and his throne as the sun before me. It shall be established forever as the moon, and as a faithful witness in heaven."—Psalms lxxxix: 3, 4, 27-29, 34-37.

As soon therefore may we expect the sun and moon to fade from the heavens, and the endless years of eternity to cease their onward march, as that the oath and covenant of God shall fail, which pledges the great and immutable Jehovah to place the royal Son of David upon his (David's) throne, and to retain him there while the sun and moon shall shine, and the ages of eternity roll on. My next witness is the Evangelical prophet Isaiah—Isa. ix: 6, 7. When wrapped in mystic vision the holy prophet saw looming up in the dim distant future the throne and kingdom of Christ, he exclaimed that he should sit " upon the throne of David, and upon his kingdom to order it, and to establish it with judgment and with justice from henceforth even for ever. The zeal of the Lord of host will perform this." The testimony of the angel Gabriel was of the same import. He affirmed that the Lord God would give unto his Son the throne of his father David, and he should reign over the house of Jacob for ever; and of his kingdom there should be no end.—Luke i: 31–33.

The next witness adduced was Christ, who assured his apostles that in the regeneration, when he should be seated upon his throne, they also should be seated upon twelve thrones judging the twelve tribes of Israel.—Matt. xix: 28. And that this is the kingdom the Father has appointed unto Christ—Luke xxii: 25–30. That great revival sermon of Peter on the day of Pentecost, which swayed the minds of thousands before it, culminated upon the immutable covenant and the oath of God, which pledged him to raise Christ from the dead that he might fulfill his oath in placing him on David's throne.—Acts ii: 30.

It was shown that the throne and kingdom of Israel, over which Zedakiah reigned, and which shall have passed through a long series of subversions, having been restored, will be given to Christ at his second advent.— Ezek., 21:25–27. It was also shown that he is the only rightful heir to David's throne and kingdom in the universe; that the two great lines of genealogy center and terminate in him. (See Matt., 1st chapter, and Luke, 3d.) It was shown that the six elements of all the kingdoms which have ever existed, will inhere in the kingdom of God. viz.: 1st, a king to rule; 2d, a royal cabinet associated with him in the rule; 3d, subjects over which they rule; 4th, territory upon which they rule; 5th, laws by which they govern; 6th, a capital from which laws are fulminated for the government of the kingdom. It has been proved, then, that Christ will be king; that all the saints of the Most High will be his kingly cabinet; that the twelve tribes of Israel restored, in conjunction with all the nations of the earth then living, will be the subjects; that the land of Canaan, in conjunction with the area of the whole earth, will be the territory; that Jerusalem upon Mount Zion will be the metropolis of the kingdom; and that the will of God, manifested through the commandments of God, will be the supreme law of the kingdom.

It was shown that the ancient kingdom of Israel was a type of the future kingdom of God; and that these six elements inhered in it. It was further shown that the four great empires of the world prefigured in outline the fifth universal kingdom of God.

In the second and seventh chapters of Daniel, five successive and universal empires have or will occupy the whole earth. These five empires will have had the six essential elements before named. They all have occupied the same territory, and have, or will exist in just two conditions, viz: first, as local; secondly as universal kingdoms.

Christ's kingdom will, as has been shown, exist first as a stone kingdom, which represents the kingdom of Israel restored; second, as a mountain kingdom, which represents the empire of the world, or the fifth universal kingdom. In reference to the time the kingdom shall be established, it has been shown—

1st. That it will be when one like unto the Son of man shall come in the clouds of heaven. Dan. 7: 13, 14.

2d. That it will be when Christ shall come in the glory of the Father and all the angels with him, and he shall set upon the throne of his glory, and all nations shall stand before him; when as the nobleman he shall return from the far country, and dispense the emoluments of honor among his faithful servants; when he shall judge the living and the dead at his appearing and kingdom. 2 Tim. 4: 1. When the seventh trump shall sound, and the kingdoms of this world shall become the kingdom of Christ, and the time when the dead shall be judged and God shall reward his saints. Rev. 11: 15, 18. When Christ, instead of being Prince of the kings of the earth, (Rev. 1: 5) shall be inaugurated as King of Kings: when the saints shall cease to be heirs and become possessors of the kingdom; (James 2: 5) when the twelve apostles shall sit upon twelve thrones, and reign with Christ; (Matt. 19: 28) all of which shall take place when Christ shall return to earth, and the time comes for the saints to possess the kingdom; for the little horn shall prevail until that time. Dan. 7: 21, 22.) Christ's kingdom will be inaugurated when the prayer our Savior taught his disciples to pray shall be answered: "Thy kingdom come, thy will be done on earth as in heaven." Amen.

www.ingramcontent.com/pod-product-compliance
Lightning Source LLC
Chambersburg PA
CBHW020906230426
43666CB00008B/1338